PRAISE F
RESOURCE IS HUMAN

'Now I'm ready. Melissa Romo's book made me feel empowered and excited to tackle the next era of work. She combines the examples, advice and expertise of others with her own insights, stories and – most importantly – tools to be a better manager, leader, and person in the hybrid/remote world. I can't wait to get going.'

Jeff Kreisler, *Author of* Dollars and Sense,
Head of Behavioral Science at JP Morgan Chase

'*Your Resource is Human* is the book 21st-century leaders and followers have been pining for. The book celebrates the liberation of empathy with an approachable prose and functional usability for leaders and followers to move forward with success. It stretches the reader with comprehensions across the human experiences of remote employment, from the deepest psychologies of depression and guilt to bread-and-butter sociology such as diversity, equity, and inclusion, with all the pragmatism of humanity in between. It has a praxis in usability for success in leadership in the new normal of today that is sensible, practical, and, above all, humane.'

Morten G. Ender, *PhD, Professor of Sociology,*
Department of Behavioural Sciences and Leadership,
United States Military Academy, West Point

'Remote and hybrid work has fundamentally disrupted what it means to be a leader, maybe more than anything ever before.

Empathy was always important to a leader's authenticity, but now it's a superpower. Leaders: this book is your cape, tie it on!'

Shawn Kanungo, *Innovation Strategist, Speaker, and Bestselling Author of* The Bold Ones

'If you've ever wanted to get inside the brain of someone who manages a dispersed team… then make it Melissa Romo's! Making remote work more "human" requires precisely the kind of real-world recommendations and diagnostic tools offered in this book.'

John Garrett, *Author of* What's Your 'And'?: Unlock the Person Within the Professional

'As leaders, we navigate a world in which change is the only constant. *Your Resource is Human* proposes a way forward. With a blend of storytelling, interviews, and research, the book deconstructs the power of human leadership and offers a tactical playbook for cultivating shared humanity. Instead of simply urging us to embrace uncertainty, it offers an optimistic perspective: understanding how we feel and why allows us to reinstall hope within our teams, reboot the system, and reignite passion and creativity. For when we do this, we unlock infinite potential.'

Archana Mohan, *Chief Operations and Technology Officer, Veritas Investment Partners*

'We live in a disrupted world where the pace of change accelerates every single day. The world of work will never be the same again. This intelligent and well-thought-through book gives us a series of detailed insights into what this really means for leaders and how to harness the opportunities remote working brings. Succinct, personal, and informative, it is a must read for all of us interested in figuring out the future.'

James Bidwell, *CEO of Springwise, Author of* Disrupt! 100 Lessons in Business Innovation

'Written by someone who has managed fully remote teams for more than ten years, *Your Resource is Human* is one of the first books that truly captures some of the challenges of building high-performing, distributed teams. Melissa's hands-on experience serves as a great guide for those still learning how to manage in an ever-changing environment.'

Gabe Karp, *Managing Director EMEA, 10up*

'This is the book we need at this moment! In the evolving world of the new normal, Melissa Romo helps us truly understand remote and hybrid work. With this in hand, leaders will be able to engage their organizations and unlock great value for both employees and employers.'

Laraine Miller, *President, Americas Region and General Manager, USA, ekaterra*

'Attention – leadership teams, boards of directors, and investors. If you are looking to differentiate your organization, grow faster than the market, and take share, then this is the book for you. Empathy is a superpower that has been diminished over the last twenty years and is now in high demand in modern remote/hybrid working environments. Melissa Romo delivers a masterclass in leading with empathy to deliver meaningful business outcomes for employees, customers, and partners. Importantly, this book delivers the HOW, not just the why, and will make you and your organizations better immediately.'

Abigail Maines, *Chief Revenue Officer, HiddenLayer and Co-Founder, fiercenow.org*

'"Imagine you're a bottle of ketchup"!! I did not expect this in a book aimed at guiding me as a leader of people working remotely, but it's these gems of wisdom, along with practical advice, that make this book essential for any leader of people working remotely. The book is so centered on humans being human, it gives you the real life of remote work and leading through it (it's not some theoretical thesis). I love the way Melissa shares the five remote-ready leadership behaviors; they are so "real" and easy to implement!! This is a fantastic book!!'

Cathal Quinlan, *Host of the* Better@Work *podcast*

'*Your Resource is Human* hit the spot in so many places, which is why I couldn't put it down. The discussion starters are going to be my Holy Grail going forward. You hear so often how people talk about legacy and how you want to be remembered, that extra meeting you took, the scrutiny you put your team under when they missed their number, but this book reminds you: "AT THE END OF YOUR CAREER, YOU WILL ONLY EVER REMEMBER THE PEOPLE." Having a framework to measure emotions for remote and hybrid workers like Depression and Guilt will help you address them as either an individual contributor or a manager. The book opens up a totally new perspective that people will find insightful, and it answers the question: "So what do I do now?" A must read for any aspiring leader.'

Sabby Gill, *CEO, Dext*

'If you work remotely, and especially if you lead remote teams, read this. By perfectly combining insight into big thoughts – empathy, guilt, paranoia, joy – with super tactical advice, Melissa Romo gives us an effective way forward to transform remote work for ourselves and for our people. She helps us understand why we feel the way we do as remote workers and then equips us with the next right actions. *Your Resource is Human* is a practical, actionable roadmap to finding more joy, meaning, and connection at work for all workers.'

Rosa Sabater, *President, Martellus LLC*

'Great to see a book that gives leaders a real insight into how to deal successfully with this tectonic plate shift to a world where remote work is an integral part of most organizations. Melissa

Romo identifies the fears, emotions, and preconceptions, why they exist, and crucially provides a practical guide on how to lead with intent, integrity, and intelligence.'

John Riordan, *Chairman, Grow Remote*

'*Your Resource is Human* is full of my favorite quality: nuance. Melissa Romo doesn't simply outline a tactical playbook for creating a remote team, but rather she details key underlying emotions every person feels, especially when working remotely, explains how and why these emotions impact human behavior and thus organizational objectives, and describes specific leadership strategies that can help people feel joyful, motivated, and invested in their teams. Her research-based approach and her storytelling style offer a reliable and engaging blueprint for how leaders can empathetically speak directly with their people and build a culture of trust and transparency that is required for any remote or hybrid work environment to thrive.'

Amanda Doyle, *Founder and Coach, Choose Better Thoughts*

'The way we think about work is evolving at speed. As leaders of people, our role in enabling a sense of belonging and connectedness in a hybrid world has never been more vital. Melissa Romo has captured the very essence, through personal experience, observation, and the development of tools and solutions, to reveal how leaders need to reframe their approach. This reframing will lead to a better-connected experience for teams and a better care of leaders themselves in this ever-evolving, complex pursuit we call work.'

Jason Rudman, *Chief Customer Officer,*
Finance of America Companies

'From the first page, this book is engaging, honest, and necessary. Not only is Melissa Romo sharing candidly about her own personal and professional journey and verbalizing elegantly the challenges of many remote and hybrid leaders, but she also then gathers and presents many stories and evidence as further illustration. She provides a step-by-step guide for others, which is accessible, practical, and can be put into action straight away. From the self-reflection scans to the conversation starters to the extensive questionnaires, the book contains a wealth of constructive tools. If you truly want to connect with empathy with your team, this book will show you how.'

Rowena Hennigan, *Remote Work Pioneer, LinkedIn Top Voice and Instructor, Founder of RoRemote*

'As a remote manager both pre-pandemic and since then, I have often thought about the challenges and merits of engaging with remote teams. By way of her remote empathy scans and leadership blueprints, Melissa Romo has succinctly articulated issues of remote work that are frequently not discussed, and clear and effective means of identifying and addressing them as a leader. I found her specific tools very practical for my everyday engagements with my team, and her stories and anecdotes also made for a quick read. Kudos for bringing life to an important leadership topic that is all too often left out of leadership conversations!'

Colleen Crino, *Chief Development Officer, IT industry*

'When the pandemic began, many of us were forced to change the way we conducted business – overnight. The decision to move to a remote work model didn't have the benefit of months of planning, a scripted rollout with accompanying policies, and support, and, as such, almost every business and leader was making it up as they went along. *Your Resource is Human* provides frameworks and tools to help you maximize the performance of your team in a world where building trust and leading with empathy are keys to success.'

Andrew Bolton, *SVP, Chief Customer Officer, Knotch*

'Melissa Romo names what we are all feeling but have not been able to express. *Your Resource is Human* is a must read for leaders who find themselves or their teams stuck with how to embrace remote and hybrid working arrangements. It provides a straightforward set of leadership behavior blueprints that identify five emotions that prevent people from doing their best work and offers specific solutions to create the conditions for people to thrive. The book is carefully researched and filled with relatable stories that paint a clear picture of this unique point in time and how much work is still needed to truly embrace our current work realities.'

Laura Schwarz, *Founder of i2 Leadership, Host of* Mojo Mondays Bootcamp *Podcast*

'*Your Resource is Human* is full of intelligent and insightful reflections on the current reality of remote working. It not only provides managers with valuable insights to help them understand the potential pitfalls when leading remote – or dispersed – teams, but it is also a powerful and up-to-date manual for leaders. Read the book and you will feel much better equipped to support your teams as they face a new form of work that looks like it's here to stay.'

Beatriz Martín-Luquero, *HR Leader Latam, Merck & Co.*

'This book provides an important tool for leaders trying to figure out how to help their teams be successful in a world where remote working is here to stay. It details the new reality we're leading teams through and expands on this framework with assessment tools and solutions that will help folks deliver authentic, empathic leadership to their teams.'

Jimm Bell, *Co-Founder, Fidem Financial*

'Today's leaders are redefining *where we work* and *how we work* all around the world. There is no blueprint, no one-size-fits-all, yet this inflection point of change will be felt by all generations to follow. *Your Resource is Human* lays out how to lead high performing teams, build trust, and inspire the best in people, all while giving them flexibility and choice.'

Amy Tomlinson, *Employee Experience and Virtual Workspace Expert*

'I knew this was going to be a helpful book to put into the world, but I was not prepared for the journey Melissa took me on. She acknowledges and explains the visceral feelings of Loneliness, Guilt, Boredom, Paranoia, and Depression. Melissa reminds us that to experience these feelings is to be human and that we can connect with each other on a deeper level when we see these feelings in others and support them to be able to thrive at work.'

Chaya Mistry, *Founder and Director, Humanly Consulting*

'In an age where "management by wandering around" is no longer possible, *Your Resource Is Human* offers a beacon of clarity for leaders managing people. Melissa's framework gives a powerful simple blueprint that decodes the leadership behaviors that are really important. It's time to put the "human" back at the heart of the workplace – and this brilliant gem of a book shows us exactly how.'

Sarah Lloyd-Hughes, *Founder and CEO of Ginger Leadership Communications and Author of* How to be Brilliant at Public Speaking

'Essential reading for every single leader! Whether leading remotely or in a hybrid way is new to you or not, you will learn something from Melissa Romo. What I love most about the book is that it is so practical with diagnostics and route maps to help you make improvements, but it also gets to the heart of the matter. An aspect of leadership is to pay attention to the emotions that our colleagues experience and respond with empathy. Thank you, Melissa Romo, for showing us how.'

Jenny Garrett OBE, *Founder, Executive Coach and Leadership Trainer*

YOUR RESOURCE IS HUMAN

HOW EMPATHETIC LEADERSHIP CAN HELP REMOTE TEAMS RISE ABOVE

MELISSA ROMO

First published in Great Britain by Practical Inspiration Publishing, 2023

© Melissa Romo, 2023

The moral rights of the author have been asserted

ISBN   9781788603942 (print)
　　　　9781788603966 (epub)
　　　　9781788603959 (mobi)

Every effort has been made to trace copyright holders and to obtain their permission for the use of copyright material. The publisher apologizes for any errors or omissions and would be grateful if notified of any corrections that should be incorporated in future reprints or editions of this book.

Want to bulk-buy copies of this book for your team and colleagues? We can customize the content and co-brand *Your Resource is Human* to suit your business's needs.

Please email info@practicalinspiration.com for more details.

Practical Inspiration
Publishing

To my parents, Rusty and Liz Tomlinson – two extraordinary humans.

And in memory of my teacher, Sigal Barsade, who taught us that emotions have a place at work.

'Could a greater miracle take place than for us to look through each other's eyes for an instant?'

– *Walden,* Henry David Thoreau

CONTENTS

FOREWORD

In 2009, I was excited and curious about how people were using the emerging online tools to collaborate remotely. I disliked working in an office myself, and I wanted to understand what kinds of companies were working remotely, how they were doing it, and how I could do it too. I came up with the idea of interviewing people as a way of getting more information. To entice people into talking to me, I told them I was writing a book. I never had any intention of actually writing a book, but, over time, interest in remote work kept growing to the point that people were messaging me regularly asking when the book would be published. I finally gave in and consolidated the tips and best practices into the *Work Together Anywhere* handbook, which was published by Wiley in 2020, just in time for the pandemic.

My own 100% remote team consists of a group of freelancers that work together voluntarily. Don't worry; I pay them! What I mean by 'voluntarily' is that there are no contracts; the amount of work varies according to the projects we take on. We work together because we want to. With this kind of business structure, relationships and trust are crucial.

I thought I was a good leader until I started researching distance leadership practices to further develop the information in my *Connected Hybrid Leader* workshop. Day to day, I ticked what I thought were the essential boxes when leading my team. Most notably, I was organized, dependable, and great with technology. I prepared for and led weekly team meetings and kept everyone updated on project statuses. And still, something was missing. While my team met regularly, we still felt siloed and separated by more than just distance. These feelings surfaced in our retrospectives: Mariah was feeling unmotivated and wasn't sure why; Tahira didn't know what Mariah was working on; I was busy with my own work. We spent a lot of time brainstorming ways to feel more like a team – more 'connected' – while maintaining the autonomy and freedom we all valued.

During this time, my friend Rowena asked if she could introduce me to Melissa. I was told she was writing a book about remote work and empathetic leadership and wanted to get my perspective on virtual collaboration practices. Of course, any friend of Rowena's is a friend of mine, so we scheduled a time to meet via video.

As we talked, I was happy to learn how aligned our views on leadership were. And I was particularly struck by Melissa's focus on empathy and care. Then I read the manuscript. And I realized why my team felt so siloed: I wasn't properly caring for them. Sure, I encourage people to take the day off when they're not feeling well, and I send an 'It's Friday!' celebration in our WhatsApp group... but as I reflected on my behavior over the past few months, I recognized that I had also forgotten my colleague's birthday. And I automated part of someone's job without telling them. Neither of these actions was intentional. But intentional or not, actions have consequences.

Working remotely requires more transparency at every level of the company. More transparency means being able to see what others are doing, understanding what success looks like for the team, knowing the financial health of the company, and being able to access information and support when necessary. Some companies are even going so far as to make everyone's salaries transparent. We want our leaders to keep the team on schedule and focused on the goals. We want to understand how our work fits into the bigger picture. And perhaps most importantly of all, we want to know that our leader cares, that they will stand up for us because we're on a team together, and that we can trust them to do the right thing when it matters.

Being a great leader is not something we achieve once and then leave behind us. Great leadership is an ongoing journey; one that requires constant effort, dedication, and a passion for motivating others. It's not enough to just be organized, dependable, and great with technology. After reading Melissa's book, I realized that properly caring for a team means getting to know them as people, understanding why they come to work to begin with, and making time to hear what they need from me, especially while we work together remotely. Building personal relationships is not something that comes naturally to me. In an effort to build more closeness, I set a recurring task for myself (using an online tool) that reminds me to check in with each member of my team. And while the method sounds mechanized and robotic, I assure you: the intention and the conversations are not.

Melissa's book takes you on an engaging, story-filled journey where she explores the five unspoken remote work emotions and offers a blueprint of core habits for empathetic remote leadership. Topics such as trust and empathy can feel very abstract, but Melissa's questionnaires, empathy scans, and discussion starters throughout the book will compel you to start improving as a leader, no matter where you are on your journey.

If you're feeling lost in this new hybrid world of working, then look no further. Melissa will walk you through the process of identifying your strengths and weaknesses so you can lead with empathy and compassion.

Lisette Sutherland
Author of *Work Together Anywhere*
Founder and Director, Collaboration Superpowers

PREFACE

I am writing this book because I have worked remotely for more than ten years, and while I have benefitted greatly from the flexibility, I have also sometimes struggled. And now I'm watching people struggle around me and not know how to talk about it. I'm watching leaders worry about productivity and the collapse of culture. I'm watching people say they want to work remotely because they prize the flexibility while not wanting to mention the downsides for fear of losing the option to work how they want. I want to help you make sense of the thousands of headlines on this topic by telling you the story of one remote worker, one remote leader: me.

Mine is both a success story and a cautionary tale. A success story because, in my most recent role working remotely for a multinational company, Sage, my remit and career have grown through several promotions and the expansion of my dispersed global team. From the standpoint of growing my career, being fully remote hasn't disadvantaged me at all. But mine is a cautionary tale because I sometimes feel marooned. I would prefer to work a few days a week in the office, but, because of personal circumstances, I live 800 miles from my company's nearest location. I also have global responsibilities, so even if I *were* in one of our company's offices, I would be separated from the rest of my team by thousands of miles and many time zones. So team separation, whether remote or not, has become a day-in and day-out reality for me. I love the flexibility and I love leading a global business, but I miss everyone, too.

I have found myself in a conundrum that I have spent years trying to resolve: how do I work far away but still stay close?

How do I stay in the job I love but contend with loneliness and isolation? I traveled often in the years before the Covid-19 pandemic, but then all of that stopped for me like it stopped for everyone, and the struggles became more acute.

I wrote this book to help leaders, including myself, get to Work 2.0, where connections are the rule, no matter where and when we work with each other.

Maybe you are contending with the same challenge – in a job you love, with flexibility you prize, but lonely and pining for togetherness and esprit de corps. Maybe you're a leader who worries about her team drifting apart and its culture dissolving, about onboarding new hires and supporting the career development of the most junior workers while offices are only half full.

Leading people remotely – keeping them connected, focused, and motivated to deliver good work – is hard. I went to business school before social media and broadband; remote leadership principles were never in the curriculum because barely anyone worked like that 20 years ago. There was no playbook when I started working remotely myself, and most of what I've learned has come through trial and error, doing it day in and day out, just like you are. That personal experience is what informs this book, combined with anecdotes from the dozens of remote workers, leaders, and experts I've interviewed and drawing on the latest research on remote and hybrid organizations.

But at its heart, this book is for practitioners, by a practitioner.

The most profound discovery I've made through my personal experience, interviews, and research is that remote work impacts us emotionally in ways that we haven't had a language to talk about. When you stay away from the office for a long period of time, which many of us did during the Covid-19 pandemic, it can feel uncomfortable to put real shoes on and walk into an office building again. Being around people feels strange. Our interpersonal skills have atrophied. Commutes were always a waste of time, but now they sometimes feel absurdly so when we can do most of the same work without the back and forth.

Working remotely means we can be sick and not tell anyone. I know because I was diagnosed with breast cancer in 2020 and remote work let me live a double life during my treatment. I underwent surgery and spent a month going to daily radiation therapy, and I was able to schedule it all around work. Physically, I could keep logging in as if nothing were happening – the scars and radiation burns were below camera level. But emotionally, I wasn't doing myself any favors by trying to carry on with business as usual. I thought about letting my team know, but I didn't want to add one more grim reality to their daily pandemic lives by telling them that their manager had cancer. But I needed empathy in the workplace more than ever, and I probably made the ordeal much harder for myself by not letting it in.

I have been a people leader for almost 30 years and have worked remotely since 2009 in all guises – from a solopreneur managing freelancers to what I do now leading a distributed team within a multinational company. In my current team, we log in to work in ten cities from London to Los Angeles. Less than 20% of my team are in the same country as I am. We speak four languages and our ages span 20- to 50-somethings. I treasure the diversity of my team in age, language, life experience, and especially – as a self-professed globalist – geography.

Every day, I am called upon to ensure that this team delivers their best work, and that they love doing it. I am called upon to provide clear direction, make decisions, allocate resources, and align and manage expectations across a complex, matrixed organization; to promote strategy and gain buy-in from my colleagues; to resolve conflicts, listen and advise, coach and support, celebrate and encourage, inspire and motivate.

It helps tremendously that I work for a company with the technology tools and the culture that make a person who is fully remote feel included and be equipped to do their best work.

When I started working fully remote in North America, I was embraced by the Colleague Success team and learned that I was part of the company's largest 'campus' in North America – the remote campus. On the occasion of any big internal event, if I can't travel to attend it, an 'event pack' gets mailed to my house with a note of thanks and excitement for the upcoming event. One year when I had trouble with my laptop, the IT team sent a replacement the same day from Atlanta to New York. We have the best collaboration tools around that let me chat, video call, share files, brainstorm, present a document, ask questions during a town hall, or participate in meetings both large and small. In short, nothing is lacking, either culturally or technologically, to enable me to be a success as a fully remote colleague.

But my epiphany is this: if you have all those things but your leaders aren't specifically skilled in how to lead hybrid and remote teams, how to connect across the miles, or how to understand the nuanced experience of working at a distance to other colleagues, then remote workforces will still struggle.

We can thank Stanford Professor of Economics Nicholas Bloom for opening the door to our understanding of remote working with his seminal experiment in 2011. His study of Chinese employees who worked remotely over the course of a nine-month period proved that working from home both improved measured productivity (up 13%) and decreased attrition (down 50%). But in a well-being survey after the experiment, 24% of participants in the remote workforce reported being lonely. And during the pandemic, when remote work was thrust upon people under extraordinary conditions, loneliness was reported as much as two-thirds of the time by people working from home. Other emotions and mindsets complicate working from home as well, and we need our leaders more than ever to be the tie that binds us. Not our technology, our leaders.

My friend Colleen Crino is a chief development officer in the IT industry. She told me about her company testing Oculus headsets and encouraging teams to use them to connect on a new level. She tried it out, played some games, and talked to the avatars (not the real people) working with her. After an hour of wearing it on her face, however, she says it just weighed too much. And she confessed that what she really wants to figure out is not how to talk to an avatar, but how to leverage what she calls 'the art of the team meeting'. She felt that the best thing she could do for her team was to be great at structuring a group meeting and getting them together more in virtual 'all hands' calls. Leading the connection with her own self, not her metaverse identity.

I hope this book can help all remote leaders find their purpose in a world of work that has never demanded more from us than it does now. Making sure that the humans can thrive as much as the work does is the last piece of the remote and hybrid working puzzle.

Let's fit that piece into place together.

Melissa Romo
Hoboken, New Jersey
April, 2023

INTRODUCTION

In the days following the terrorist attacks on September 11, 2001, the employees of the American Express Company were fully displaced to temporary offices. The headquarters building of American Express was across the street from the World Trade Center in Lower Manhattan, and for more than a year following the event, nobody would be able to work there. A friend of mine told me the story of coming to work in those first numbing days when all of New York City, when all the world, was in a state of shock.

She took the subway from the Upper West Side of Manhattan to a ferry that would take her to an office across the Hudson River in New Jersey, where the company had set up a temporary office. The commute was crowded with people handing out missing person flyers. The flyers had the pictures, names, and identifiable information of a loved one they hadn't seen since the morning of Tuesday, September 11. *She was wearing a blue pantsuit. He had a tattoo on his left arm. He was last seen on the 102nd floor of the South Tower. She is missing a molar on the lower left side of her jaw. Please call if you have any information.* The collective effort everyone was making to believe that the deceased were actually only missing made those first days and weeks heartbreaking in a way that is hard to describe.

Every day, my friend had to pass missing person flyers taped by the thousands to every fence and lamp post. When she arrived at the ferry dock in New Jersey every morning, the company's CEO, Ken Chenault, was there to greet his employees. He spoke to them. He asked them how they were feeling. He asked what he could do for them. He empathized with their traumatic journey to get to work. *He was with them in that grim commute.* She has never forgotten how much he cared.

When I began working for American Express in 2003, employees had only just started to return to the company's Lower Manhattan headquarters, across the street from the vacant footprint of what had been the two World Trade Center towers. From my desk on the 28th floor, I could look down into the vast container that engineers called 'the bathtub' because it had been designed to both support the enormous towers and keep water from the New York harbor and Hudson River at bay. The bathtub had steel plugs along its wall that looked like a balding doll's head after time and tantrums had shed its hair. The plugs had held thick braids of steel wire that ran to the top of the buildings and anchored the towers like a suspension bridge. It was those braids of steel wire that eventually pulled the buildings to the ground when their steel frames melted and the tension at the top gave way.

On the anniversary of September 11 each year, the company invited employees to work from home, something that was barely done in the years before broadband. On those anniversaries, families gathered in huge numbers around the bathtub. A platform was erected on the edge of it, and, one by one, the name of each person who perished was read aloud by a loved one. Many of the voices were of very young children who had lost their parents. From where I sat behind triple-paned glass, their tiny voices echoed like the tin sound from the speaker of an old radio. In 2003, I didn't know about the ceremony that would be taking place so I didn't work from home; without the right tools and technology back then it would have been more of an inconvenience. So I came to work and sat on the 28th floor, and from 8am to almost 11am I listened to the tiny voices of children reading out their parents' names. It was hard to listen to, the heartbreak all around us so palpable. In future years, I worked from home that day.

The Covid-19 pandemic was not a single day's trauma, but it was a similarly insidious tragedy, claiming the lives of millions of people globally under heartbreaking circumstances. There is nobody the pandemic didn't touch. At work, the pandemic made us all feel raw. Conversations between managers and teams cut closer to emotions than ever as life and work blended together at home and life for some people took grim turns. A macabre routine began for me as a leader: to have life and death issues impacting the people who worked for me, and needing to have a solution in the moment that was compassionate to the person but would still keep business going. Over and over. How to keep the work from slipping but still take care of the people. As a manager, I was exhausted trying to do this right. I'm not sure I always did.

On any given day, one of my employees would let me know that someone in their family was in the hospital. Or that their husband was isolating in one bedroom and their children in another, with my employee delivering food to their doors in between conference calls. Or a parent was hanging close to death in an ICU and could my employee have the afternoon off to stand outside the hospital in case the parent was well enough to be wheeled to a viewing corridor with windows. Or letting me know they would be offline for a few hours because they were going to wait in line with hundreds of people to get a vaccine. There was no leadership playbook for what the pandemic was doing to employees and companies. Just like Ken Chenault had no leadership playbook for September 11.

In the case of September 11, and also following the terrorist bombings in London and Madrid, many leaders stepped forward to support their employees in extraordinary ways. During the pandemic, companies did extraordinary things too: mental health became okay to talk about; some companies gave unlimited holiday; well-being perks such as meditation apps and wellness resources became table stakes in any job.

But why does it need to take a traumatic event for us to remember that we are humans and to treat each other that way? Another leader at American Express was well known for carrying around an index card of the company's performance indicators. One of those indicators was the number of 'swipes' of employee badges at the lobby turnstiles. Utilization of real estate is certainly an important financial indicator to keep track of, but one can quickly see how measuring 'bodies in the building' can start to dehumanize a workforce.

Post-pandemic, attendance-taking is all the rage. Tracking swipes has reportedly become a popular tactic of many financial firms and many other large companies, with dashboards of each team's swipe performance delivered to leaders. Managers are expected to spend their time controlling the number of times an employee walks into the building. And if it's two days instead of three, managers are expected to do something about it. I've asked corporate leaders in my circle who receive these reports every week if they know what they are supposed to do with them and they are at a loss. Whether they ignore the reports or take action – though the action is unclear – they say they will lose either way. The company's reprimand is the frying pan; the employee's revolt is the fire.

Despite mandates from leaders such as Elon Musk that people need to come back to the office, office occupancy rates at the time of writing, as measured by security badge swipes into offices, had plateaued at 42% across a ten-city average in the US, according to the office security solutions provider Kastle Systems. Six of the ten markets surveyed actually reported *declining* office occupancy rates, including Austin, Dallas, and New York City.

Susan Sobbott, the former President of Global Commercial Services at American Express, talked to me about the company's long history of adopting remote work and the struggle at that company, and at many others, to accept it. The company began setting up home offices for sales and support teams as early as the 1990s, as part of a real-estate cost-savings strategy. Susan herself worked several days a week from home starting in the late 1990s, something her remote manager – from his home in Boston – encouraged her to do.

Susan went on to create the Project Resource Team at American Express in the early 2000s as a benefit to employees who wanted to work remotely. I was one of those employees, and I talk about my reasons for *not* taking advantage of the PRT in Chapter 3 on guilt. Despite the fact that the PRT was available to thousands of employees, only a dozen – all women – actually took part. Nevertheless, Susan credits the PRT with helping to lift employee sentiment across the board. Even if an employee didn't take advantage, just the existence of the program made employees feel better about work and sent a message from the company that said, 'We care'. And yet inequities were unavoidable. Susan told me about an instance where she had to demote someone who needed to relocate across the country and be a permanent remote employee. Going remote sometimes meant going backwards, and sometimes it still does.

Fortunately, many companies around the world made a wide range of gestures that said 'We care' during the pandemic. I don't think it's going too far to say we found our collective humanity during the pandemic because of the extraordinary circumstances, especially in our workplaces. We had to do whatever it took to get things done. We showed up, whatever that looked like. While it was stressful, it also gave us autonomy, agency, and humility. This intense daily problem-solving around the messy contours of our chaotic and threatened well-being reconnected us to what makes us human and to our fundamental needs and responsibilities, and it connected us more to each other. It became such a cliche to say, 'We're in this together', but we really were.

The thing is, we are humans every day, not just when the world is crashing down on us. But now that the pandemic is no longer a forcing mechanism for autonomy and agency, I worry we will go backwards and lose all of that beautiful where-there's-a-will-there's-a-way camaraderie. I don't want that, and I assume if you're reading this book, then you don't either. But I assume you also want a game plan for how to manage remotely with intention, not desperation.

When the pandemic happened and everyone abruptly flipped to at-home work where they could, I was struck by how many people told me they hadn't heard from their leader in weeks. Companies were helping employees but leaders had disappeared. Why? This was one of the questions I wanted to find an answer to in this book. What is the role of the leader in traumatic times, in regular times, as a human being leading other human beings? And with remote and hybrid work likely to become more the norm, how can leaders create, build, and nurture connections that will impact not only employee engagement but also business performance for the long term?

Who this book is for

This book is for leaders who are feeling lost about how to make remote and hybrid work *work*. From talking with those close to senior executives, I get a sense that they're not comfortable about remote and hybrid work, but they don't feel as if they are allowed to say so. There are some notable exceptions where CEOs have publicly shared their disaffection over remote work, their statements often followed by resignations, petitions, and social media turmoil.

You have likely seen the labor statistics that make clear there is no putting the remote work genie back in her bottle. It's too much in demand by the people you are hiring. People are demanding work that's worth doing in a way that makes sense to do it. According to the US Bureau of Labor Statistics, November 2021 saw resignations peak at 4.5 million people, almost 30% higher than November 2019 and the highest single month of resignations since the data collection began in 2000. Research from the US-based think tank Pew Research Center in February 2022 told us why: 63% of people who resigned were looking for better pay and advancement, but, close behind, 57% said they felt disrespected at work and 45% said their job lacked flexibility. Add to this an insight from a 2021 survey by Gartner: 65% of people surveyed said the pandemic has even made them rethink the role of work in their lives. Something akin to 'life's too short'.

But you're savvy, and, even though it makes you uncomfortable, you know that supporting how, where, and even why people work is a management dance step you are going to need to master if you want access to talent. But I want to go one better than just helping you choke remote work down like a dry crust of bread. I want you to see it for what it really is – opportunity. Opportunity to hire who you want, where you want. Opportunity to fill the ranks of your company with geographically diverse talent. Opportunity to bring alive the creativity and discretionary effort of the people who work for you because they know you care. You aren't just hiring people to take up space, you're hiring people to help you *win*. And I want you to learn that connections across and through remote teams do not come via technology, they come via humans. Connections come via you.

I wrote this book for everyone who manages people working physically alone in a remote or hybrid arrangement. We call it 'remote working', but what it really is is working alone, in a private space, with the professional world on the other side of a ten-inch screen. My teenage sons call my world of work 'the matrix': *Mom's back in the matrix again.* Being in the matrix does something to the way a person feels, works, and acts, and this book will help you understand those human dynamics and lead you through them.

Many books will help you become a better leader of remote and hybrid teams through better project management practices, productivity techniques, and an ever-growing array of technology tools. But even with the best remote technology in the world, if your leaders don't know how to build human connections alongside the tech, then you don't win. Your remote leadership is needed in ways you have likely never imagined. Your team needs to know you care, especially when you are separated by distance.

There are instructive lessons in leadership, especially remote leadership, from the renowned horse trainer Pat Parelli. Parelli teaches according to a methodology he calls 'natural horsemanship'. The principle is that horsemanship can be obtained naturally through communication, understanding, and psychology instead of mechanics, fear, and intimidation.

Think about that: communication, understanding, and psychology instead of mechanics, fear, and intimidation. There is so much in that principle that we can apply to the current leadership struggle over remote work, so much that can help us reframe leadership from the demands of industrial-era shareholder capitalism to 21st-century stakeholder capitalism with humans at the heart.

Parelli has been teaching natural horsemanship for 40 years using the techniques of Language, Leadership, and Love. He uses these techniques to teach what he calls the 'unteachable' of human and horse behavior: *feel, timing, and balance.*

Feel, timing, and balance are what are needed for a human and a horse to achieve a goal together – jump a fence, race round a track at breakneck speed, break away from the pack to cross the wire in the lead. No language can pass between horse and human. There can only be *feel, timing, and balance* that are perfectly understood with no explanation, coercion, or control. *Feel, timing, and balance* enable success.

Parelli's philosophy reminds us about the potential of connection that can happen between two beings, if those beings are open to the connection. Such a connection engenders trust. True leadership, the kind that makes a CEO stand at a ferry terminal to console his workforce, is part of the unteachable mysticism of leadership. I don't want to imply that your employees are horses, but Parelli's insights are too good not to share. I love how Parelli sums up how essential caring is to his natural horsemanship methodology: *A horse doesn't care how much you know until it knows how much you care.*

In the spirit of Parelli's beliefs about connection, Susan Sobbott shared this reflection with me: 'Energy flows through us and to others. If you are going to create energy and dynamism, you've got to spread that energy. And spreading that energy only happens through connection.'

The successful leader of a remote team is someone who finds within them the patience, candor, and grace to care through true connections. They know how to communicate enough, maintain a steady presence, ask the right questions, and still navigate the boundaries of privacy. Every remote worker needs something slightly different. A skilled remote leader knows how to keep expectations of performance in their right place while creating an organizational culture in which all hands will find the pump should one pair of hands momentarily fail.

If you've ever ended a video call with someone who works for you and had that nagging feeling *Something seems off...* then this book is for you. You are already open to making a connection between yourself and the other humans you work with. This book will give you the blueprints to take advantage of that open door. Getting the best out of people hasn't changed, but the people trying to do their best have.

How to use this book

+ **In Part One, we will delve into the five emotional pitfalls of remote and hybrid work** and understand the dynamics of each in a remote context: boredom, depression, guilt, paranoia, and loneliness. I'll be honest with you: it doesn't make for light reading. But this book will help you understand the special patterns of these emotions for remote employees, how they get in the way of connections, why they occur, and how to spot them. The silver lining is that each one has an emotional counterpoint that any leader can bring to bear.

+ **In Part Two, we will master the five remote-ready leadership behavior blueprints** that form the core habits of an empathetic remote leader: checking in, communicating with optimism, building trust, setting boundaries, and managing performance. These behaviors are organized around the Remote Leadership Wheel™, which will help you see how each behavior interconnects and aids empathy.

+ **Each section starts with a diagnostic tool.** In Part One, the tool will help you take a pulse of your and your employees' emotions and mindsets when it comes to remote work. In Part Two, it will help you assess how ready you are for remote leadership, and where you most need to build your skills.

+ **The book ends with conversation starters and leadership blueprint summaries**, quick references you can refer to at a glance to recall concepts from the book, kickstart conversations, and apply the remote-ready leadership behavior blueprints that suit any situation.

Chapter 1

BETWEEN ONE WORK WORLD AND THE NEXT

*E*arly in the Covid-19 pandemic, the Indian author Arundhati Roy wanted us to know we were facing a rare opportunity. She wrote an essay in which she declared that pandemics were 'portals, a gateway between one world and the next'. At such a time, we can insist on holding onto the world we knew before, or we can arrive at the portal and 'walk through it, ready to imagine another world'.

Both *the way we work* and *the way we lead* are standing like siblings at the threshold of a portal leading to a different world of work. Leadership theories stretch back for hundreds, if not thousands, of years, but I believe we have reached an inflection point that will either bring out a new era of enlightened leadership or send us back to our industrial-age trenches. Which direction it will be is largely in the hands of you, the person holding this book.

At the time of writing, remote and hybrid work is for the most part no longer mandatory as it was during the Covid-19 pandemic. We have entered the golden moment of choice in work design, which should make both employers and employees hopeful for the future. Adam Grant, bestselling author and organizational psychologist at the Wharton School of Business, suggested in a 2022 interview that there is reason to be hopeful we've turned a corner in leadership: 'One of the few silver linings of the pandemic is that more people at a leadership and management level are starting to recognize that if you do not care about people's quality of life, you don't get quality work.'

Employees have proven that they can work effectively from home for jobs that are suited to it, but there's still a struggle over remote and hybrid work and how companies want to adopt it, if at all. What is the struggle about? It is about breaking with habit, tradition, and culture, but it may also be partly about losing control – seeing people in the flesh feels like the way to control what they are doing. And if seeing means controlling, then not seeing means everything is out of control. It's tempting to want to brush control aside as a 'bad' behavior that is at odds with vulnerability and connection-building, but control plays an important role in business, too.

Control underpins all business strategy and decision-making. I learned at an early stage in my career that you never communicate a problem to a superior unless you have a solution to go along with it. Risk is always communicated alongside actions to mitigate that risk. As a business leader, you are expected to be in control of outcomes at all times. Not a week goes by that I am not asked the question: 'What is the risk to the business if we do/don't do that?' Controlling risk is at the core of building stakeholder value and delivering consistent products and services to customers. There's no other way to do that except through control.

However, if we accept that control is necessary, there's still another way we can think about remote work. John Riordan, a former executive at Virgin Atlantic, Shopify, and Apple, and now the Chairman of Grow Remote, an award-winning social enterprise focused on supporting local remote employment, offered a great framing for the control conundrum: we need to separate controlling the work from controlling the humans doing the work. We can predict and control the outcomes we want, of course. But how the humans achieve those outcomes can be more up to them than it was before the pandemic.

John's advice to leaders struggling with control is to trust your hiring decisions: 'You have hired excellent employees, you have assigned them a task or a body of work – now let them do it. By all means, check in and encourage. I'm a firm believer in "trust but verify" – but the secret sauce of trust is to trust your judgment in hiring that individual and assigning them the task.'

As a leader, ask yourself: are you trying to control the work or the humans doing the work? How differently would you see remote work if you were focused on controlling the work rather than the humans doing it?

It won't be easy to make remote and hybrid work a success, but here's why it's worth it:

1. The most important reason we want it to work is that employees are not just asking for it, they are demanding it. Most employees when surveyed would like the choice to work when and where they want, if the requirements of the job allow for that choice. If we as employers decide we *don't* want to give job seekers any choice, we will see our pool of prospective employees diminish.

2. Creating a company in which productivity is not dependent on physical location gives employers more options. Suddenly a job can be filled with the perfect candidate, regardless of where they live. Relocation packages may largely become a thing of the past if employees are allowed to stay put for a new job. That said, navigating taxes, benefits, and work practices in different countries is an evolving challenge. Sarah Hawley, founder and CEO of the remote staffing tech start-up Growmotely and author of *Conscious Leadership*, sees the future of work more like a

contractor model, giving professionals the freedom to choose where they live and pay taxes. She already sees that work is being uncoupled from nation states, and this is a huge shift that countries and governments will need to accept and make provision for. And if another large-scale crisis caused by a natural disaster, pandemic, war, or climate change arises, and we can be sure it will, then a company that has uncoupled its workforce from its workplace, whether all or part of the time, can be much nimbler. When remote work wins, business continuity wins. We learned this principle on 9/11 and it hasn't changed.

3. Remote and hybrid work is a win for wellness. With the right organizational design and skilled leadership, there is now a significant body of research to prove that remote work makes employees happier, reduces stress, enhances work-life balance, and increases job control. Remote work holds the promise of many benefits that can make our workforces more robust both now and in the future… but the big caveats are the first two points I mentioned here: organizational design and skilled leadership. If employees are battling in their quest for remote or hybrid work success, the promise of remote work will remain unfulfilled.

4. Getting good at remote and hybrid work means we can create a more sustainable global economy by effectively reducing our need to move around – both short-distance commutes and long-distance business trips. Remote work doesn't automatically lower a company's carbon footprint, because there are additional impacts such as streaming video calls and home office heating and cooling. But if a company makes a conscious choice to compensate remote work with reduced travel,

hybridizing all meetings, it can mean that teams travel less as a matter of company policy because remote collaboration is openly accepted and nurtured. When leaders are able to empathetically engage their employees from a distance, it means off-sites can happen once or twice a year, not quarterly or even more often. Remote work holds a lot of promise for companies seeking a net-zero future. You can find more information on this in Appendix A: Low carbon strategies for remote work.

5. Remote and hybrid work can support our diversity and inclusion efforts by creating opportunities for new segments of the workforce to enter the job market, but there is one important warning: employees who choose to work remote or hybrid risk exclusion through 'proximity bias'. Proximity bias is the advantage given to people who work in the office rather than from home. Removing proximity bias has to do with giving a remote employee the same access to information, people, culture, influence, pay, and career progression that a person has when they work in a company office. Diversity and inclusion teams are paying a lot of attention to proximity bias; search volume about the topic on Google has doubled in 2022. Concerning access to jobs, many countries are seeing the advent of new work-from-home laws, and, in the US, we are beginning to see legal cases brought against employers under the Americans with Disabilities Act mandating that 'telework' should be granted as a reasonable accommodation for someone to be able to work. These 'telework' requests were often swiftly declined in the pre-pandemic world, but now courts are determining that employers must give them due consideration. You can find more information in Appendix B: Diversity and inclusion considerations for remote work.

I believe in remote work, whether fully remote or hybrid remote, because people want it and have shown they can make it work, and I believe in the possibilities of people. But remote work is broken. It's broken because many organizations and their leaders seem as if they may slip back to the world of remote work the way it was before we were all forced to do it: when remote work was the exception not the rule, when it was acceptably stigmatized, when it was the domain of the working parent or the person who had presumably opted out of their career in favor of prioritizing other domains in their life. The remote person didn't really count, and the work they did wasn't really work. I was a remote worker during that era, and it was the lowest point in my career. People dismissing what I did at home as not being 'real work' impacted my confidence, my self-esteem, and even my overall outlook on life. That's no model to go back to.

There are many leaders today who believe that remote work is business's fastest route to the best, most diverse talent. Matt Mullenweg, founder of the distributed web design and development company Automattic, famously designed his company from its founding in 2005 to be fully distributed. He prefers the term 'distributed' over 'remote', believing that the latter implies a headquarters where some people are located, and those who aren't are labeled 'remote' and considered to be separated at a distance. It creates an 'us and them' dynamic. Mullenweg believes that distributed work is important because 'talent is evenly distributed around the world but opportunity is not'. Now more than 15 years old, Automattic is valued at over $7 billion, and its workforce has been distributed since day one. The company's nearly 2,000 employees work wherever and whenever they want.

Darren Murph, Head of Remote at the remote-first company GitLab, published a manifesto on his LinkedIn profile declaring the value of remote work: 'I believe remote work can reverse rural depopulation, make communities less transitory, and spread opportunity to underserved areas. I believe all-remote is the purest form of remote work, where every individual is afforded a level playing field.'

Warren Buffett's philosophy of the 'ovarian lottery' says something similar to Mullenweg – that his success was due in large part to the economic system he was born into – in his case in Omaha, Nebraska, and not Bangladesh. He won, as he called it, the 'ovarian lottery'. Had he only arrived in the world as a member of a more impoverished economy, he never would have achieved the success he enjoyed in his life. Location mattered back then; it doesn't need to now.

And recently, actor and entrepreneur Ryan Reynolds asserted that creative industries need to look further afield for diverse talent, not just within a stone's throw of the Hollywood sign or Madison Avenue. He co-founded Creative Ladder with the partnership of Deloitte to help underrepresented talent everywhere train for and obtain creative marketing jobs.

These examples underscore the fact that decoupling our workforce from our workplace can unblock the limitations facing people and companies who are not on New York's Wall Street, in London's Canary Wharf, Johannesburg's Sandton, or Shanghai's Pudong. Old limitations will disappear if only we have the courage to walk through the portal in front of us.

Empathy as a tool

Because working remotely evokes complex emotions and mindsets that we are still learning about, the five leadership behavior blueprints are focused on empathizing with those emotions and taking action as a leader by using tactics to help counterbalance them.

The Greater Good Science Center, part of the University of California, Berkeley, explains that 'emotion researchers generally define empathy as the ability to sense other people's emotions, coupled with the ability to imagine what someone else might be thinking or feeling'. These two types are also referred to as 'affective empathy' and 'cognitive empathy'.

Researchers explain that empathy's purpose is to inspire compassionate action. It's the spark of recognizing universal human experience that gets us to help one another, that helps us feel connected no matter what our other differences might be. We will use the purpose of empathy – *compassionate action* – to guide us in our Leadership Blueprints in Part Two.

Emotions and empathy can be powerful tools, and they are coming into their own in business now more than ever. In 2021, the consulting firm Ernst & Young published their first-ever *Empathy in Business Survey*. Across 1,000 employed Americans at all job levels, over 80% of respondents felt that empathy resulted in better leadership, enabled trust, and led to greater productivity.

The primatologist Frans de Waal, who has studied empathy in primates, believes that emotions transcend rules and defy ideology. Empathy expands the definition of the group to which we see ourselves belonging. Empathy explains how Oskar Schindler defied his ideological and political group to keep Jews out of concentration camps during World War II; because of his empathy, he saw himself as part of a wider, more important group: human beings.

In an online quiz taken by more than 180,000 people worldwide, the Greater Good Science Center has been able to measure the degree to which people possess the two kinds of empathy – affective and cognitive. The aggregate results of their survey revealed that affective empathy is more present than cognitive and slightly more common amongst women and older respondents. If you want to take the quiz yourself you can find it on the center's website.[1] I scored 88 out of 110 and was high on affective empathy with medium cognitive empathy. How about you?

---

[1] https://greatergood.berkeley.edu/quizzes/take_quiz/empathy

The pandemic brought emotions and empathy to the forefront in new ways when McKinsey & Company created what they called the 'Emotion Archive'. This was a global research study to examine how Covid-19 was changing people's lives and livelihoods, and it was entirely based on emotions. McKinsey's study resulted in an 'Emotion Index' that showed that people the world over were feeling many of the same emotions to the same degree, especially acceptance and apprehension. Emotions so defined and united us during the pandemic that this revered firm decided to codify how that happened.

Prior to the pandemic, the study of empathy and leadership owes much to the research of the American psychologist Peter Salovey. He, along with David Caruso and John Mayer, developed the Mayer-Salovey-Caruso Emotional Intelligence Test (MSCEIT) in 2000. It measures a person's ability to employ four aspects related to emotions: perceiving emotions, using emotions, understanding emotions, and managing emotions.

Using the research underpinning the MSCEIT test as a basis, the psychologist Daniel Goleman popularized the importance of emotional intelligence, or EQ, in his landmark 1995 bestselling book *Emotional Intelligence: Why It Can Matter More Than IQ*. Goleman's book laid down the gauntlet in popular management dialogue: the smartest person in the room was not the smartest person in the room. Not anymore. Emotions mattered, possibly even more.

Empathy empowers people to apply creative thinking. Consider how critical creative thinking is to business – problem-solving, competitive strategy, communication, innovation. A UK-based study evaluated whether or not empathy improved creativity. Two cohorts of school children were given a design assignment. One cohort was told to design according to their usual design techniques; the other was told to think about other people while they created their design. The group told to think about other people showed a 78% increase in creativity as measured by the standard Torrance Test of Creative Thinking.

We can also see empathy applied in the approach of Design Thinking. Design Thinking is a now common methodology that guides the development of products, customer experiences, and technology user interfaces. One of the core principles of Design Thinking is the requirement that the designer must empathize with the user and put the human at the center. To prove the value of this kind of human-centered design approach, the Design Management Institute bundled 16 companies together into what it calls a Design Value Index (DVI). These 16 companies meet strict design criteria that have user-centricity and empathy as core principles. From 2005 to 2015, the companies in the DVI showed a 211% return over the S&P 500.

In sum, when empathy is activated, it drives employee engagement, retention, innovation, creativity, and even stock market performance.

But, for some reason, 68% of CEOs in Businessolver's 2021 *State of Workplace Empathy* report said they have trouble actually *being* empathetic – they actually feel they will be less respected. *Yes, it's important. No, we don't know how to do it, and we even think it will hurt our standing.* Ugh.

Laura Schwarz, an executive coach and founder and CEO of the firm i2 Leadership, says that executives have huge blind spots when it comes to empathy. Many will profess to be empathetic, but, in truth, they aren't. They will see an example of poor management and quickly say, 'That's not me.' But of course it often is, and it's a gap they can't recognize in themselves because they are operating with these blind spots. Laura says that blind spots are where our actions and our intentions are misaligned.

Most leaders have the best of intentions and want to be empathetic leaders, but if their actions don't reflect those intentions, they aren't having the impact they want. Leaders lack the discomfort, the 'friction', that helps empathy emerge because everyone in the organization is flexing to *their* needs. This means that employees don't feel they can express their true concerns and fears. So while many employees around the leader may be feeling a level of discomfort about something that requires their empathy, the discomfort and need for empathy doesn't manage to register for the leader.

As a leader, you have to delegate many things, but empathy can't be one of them. Empathy needs to be your job #1, and it can only come personally from you. Here's why: a 2020 study from Catalyst showed that senior leaders had even more impact on business performance through empathy than direct managers. If you sit in the C-suite, then pay attention! Catalyst's survey across 900 employees in the US showed that 61% reported being often or always innovative at work and 76% reported being engaged *when their senior leadership was empathetic.* This compares to 47% and 67% on the same questions with an empathetic *direct manager.*

The good news is that remote and hybrid work can actually *help you* with empathy. As a leader, you will likely learn things about the people working for you remotely that you would never learn from them if you were in the office. Sounds ironic I know, but when we are remote, we are often alone in our personal space, surrounded by the stuff of home. More of our personal selves has a chance to be expressed, both the good and the bad. This became clear to Beatriz Martín-Luquero, HR leader for Merck & Co. in Latin America. When she reflects on remote work during the pandemic, she says it began to sink in for her that she is working with people, not employees. She recalls the feeling on video calls of entering people's homes, meeting their families, seeing the plants and décor behind them. 'I *know* them now', she says. She felt she got to know people so much better through remote work, and empathy became easier.

I believe empathy comes from within a leader's deep sense of self. Nothing could have been more powerful to American Express's employee engagement than Ken Chenault greeting employees at the ferry after 9/11. But I'm sure that's not why he did it. Connecting with his workforce on an empathetic level

– commuting that commute with them – was just the human thing to do.

Men can empathize, too

In 2022, NBA star, businessman, and author Carmelo Anthony interviewed Ken Chenault for his podcast *What's in Your Glass?* During their conversation, Ken reflects on his own leadership style over a long and legendary career. Not surprisingly, empathy is the first thing he talks about: 'You have to be both compassionate and decisive', he explains. 'People will say, "If you're compassionate, you're a softie." But at the end of the day as a leader, you want to capture people's hearts and minds. So yes, *I do* want to be empathetic.'

In Businessolver's CEO survey, you can be assured that the vast majority of respondents were older men. This is because 95% of the CEOs appointed globally are men, and men outnumber women at the CEO level by 17 to 1. So why is empathy so hard, especially for senior male leaders? One reason is that men and women have been conditioned to display emotions to different degrees. In fact, there is a kooky backstory on men and empathetic leadership.

One of the earliest studies of empathetic leadership was made by the psychologist William Moulton Marston in his 1928 book *The Emotions of Normal People*. This was almost 70 years before we would begin formally codifying 'emotional intelligence' as a human trait on a par with, or, as the author Daniel Goleman would claim in 1995, even more important than, IQ. In his book, Marston makes an exhaustive study of human emotions, which became the basis of the well-known personality inventory called DISC (Dominance, Influence, Steadiness, and Compliance), which I'm sure many of you have taken. (I am an 'Influencer' with 'Dominant' leanings. You?)

I was surprised to see where Marston ended his book. He describes what he calls 'love leadership', which has four characteristics that bear all the hallmarks of 'empathetic leadership':

1. the capacity to feel and express one's own love/emotion towards others;
2. material self-sufficiency such that a person doesn't have to submit to those with access to wealth;
3. the wisdom and insight to understand the range of emotions in others;
4. the capacity to inspire others to feel and follow their emotions.

Marston concluded that, in 1928, *there wasn't a person alive who possessed all of these characteristics.* A woman couldn't be a 'love leader' because she lacked all of the characteristics apart from the first one. Men, on the other hand, would never be able to achieve the first characteristic because they lacked the essential biological trigger: menstruation. Marston couldn't reconcile that the capacity to feel and express love and emotion to others was anything more than a case of gender-specific biology.

Marston also described how men acted primarily on what he called 'appetite' not 'love', and the two could not co-exist. Appetite was about desire and satisfaction, particularly as it related to acquiring wealth, property, and status. A person who had developed power through the course of his life by acting on appetite would suffer 'appetite failure' if he began acting on love. So you see the quandary for men. You can satisfy your appetite or you can love, but you can't do both. You can control or connect, but not both.

And if you don't think this has gotten kooky enough… In addition to being the author of the DISC personality inventory, Marston was also the inventor of the lie detector test (heavily influenced by his wife's observations about blood pressure) and the creator of the comic book character Wonder Woman (heavily influenced by his wife as well).

So the next time you are watching *Wonder Woman*, think about her creator and his conviction that men would never be able to lead with love because of their biological shortcomings.

As truly bizarre as this early interpretation of empathetic leadership by genders is, we really haven't moved on very much, and that *State of Workplace Empathy* report is the proof. Men are still stuck. But guys, I want you to know I believe you have it in you. I believe this because I saw it with my own eyes outside a church in Virginia.

On May 23, 1992, we buried my dad in the cemetery of a clapboard Civil War-era church in Virginia, not far from the graves of Union and Confederate soldiers. Dad was only 46 years old when he died. The funeral was attended by our entire family, many friends, and salespeople who had faced off against him in the rarefied and fiercely competitive world of private aircraft sales. Almost all of these salespeople were men in middle age.

Everyone stood with us around his gravesite as his casket was lowered into the ground. My mother, brother, and I each threw one clump of cool, red Virginia earth onto the top of the casket. When I finished throwing my clump, I turned around and was encircled by middle-aged men in dark suits who, one by one, offered me condolences. One man hugged me, and, as he did, I felt his body quake. He was crying. The next man hugged me, and his body quaked, and the next, and the next. I had never seen an adult man cry before, except in the movies. I had never seen my own father cry before. And now I was surrounded by dozens of men, all unable to control their grief.

I knew they were crying in part because a man their age had suddenly died and they had just watched his body be lowered into the ground. It had to be sobering for them, too close for comfort. But you don't openly weep in front of strangers for that reason; you go home and have a stiff drink and try to pay more attention to your doctor's health advice. They were weeping because my dad had connected to each of them in a deeply important way. They were vulnerable there, with me, at my father's graveside, because he had been vulnerable with them, and now that vacuum of empathetic connection was overwhelming them.

I never forgot that day. I never forgot the sight of men weeping for another man they had worked with. It made an impact on me, and I truly believe the story of that moment has been waiting 30 years to find its way into this book. It showed me that men in business could feel vulnerable with each other. Despite all of the conditioning that men experience about feeling and showing emotion, at a certain point, emotion can find its way to the surface.

It shouldn't take a sudden death for men to feel comfortable showing their authentic feelings. Men have had it in them all along. And now that the world is confronting us with so many existential threats simultaneously – declining health, war, planetary collapse – there has never been a better time to let that authentic empathy out.

In her seminal TED Talk and 2019 Netflix special *Call to Courage*, Brené Brown teaches that to be vulnerable you have to give up control and the 'predictability of outcomes'. An honest and deep connection between two people can't happen if either one of them insists on control. It can be easy to see why vulnerability and connection are so hard to achieve at work – conventional business theory that is grounded in maximizing shareholder value requires control and predictability. Without it, we wouldn't trust placing our money in a company's stock.

But remote work needs connection. It needs leaders who are building connection *on purpose*, as methodically as they execute on business strategy or track ROI, EBITDA, or ARR. And empathy must be present for connection to happen, an empathy that comes from being comfortable with deep vulnerability.

Speaking of Brené, this might be a good moment to insert an apology. In her wonderful book *Dare to Lead*, she recounts how a student asked her for a decision tree for empathy. She says decision trees for empathy don't work because every human being and every situation is different. The only way you can be authentically empathetic is to connect and pay attention.

With apologies to Brené, what you'll find in Part Two of this book is basically a decision tree in the form of a wheel – the Remote Leadership Wheel™. I decided that a decision tree (or wheel, in this case) was the best way for me to help you turn your empathy into compassionate action. The wheel is made up of the five remote work emotions, five counterpoint emotions, and five leadership behavior blueprints. Empathy will help you connect with your employee where they are and understand how they're feeling. Then the blueprints are your plans for compassionate action, and they are designed to help you kickstart connection and conversation. Emotions are difficult, even more so in a work setting, but they are so necessary and even *useful*. They will be there whether we acknowledge them or not, and we get so much more engagement if we do.

Imagine you're a bottle of ketchup

OK, all that stuff about empathy is a lot to digest. You might be thinking: *I can't be vulnerable, or emotional, or show love at work. Are you crazy!?* Let me help you off the ledge. Let's talk about ketchup.

The Heinz company used the product development technique I mentioned before, Design Thinking, to redesign their bottles of ketchup. Empathy was a key tool to help them improve on the package design. Their customers had a problem – the ketchup was hard to pour. It was so hard to pour that parents never let their kids handle the bottle themselves. A simple condiment involving a huge amount of intervention to use.

Heinz was only able to understand this by putting themselves in their customer's shoes, by empathizing, through watching their customers use the product. They observed all manner of shaking the bottle, banging the back of it with the palm of the hand, and excavating dribbles of ketchup with the blade of a knife. After making these observations, Heinz realized that what was giving their customers trouble was gravity, and there was an easy way to fix that. They decided to revise the bottle design so that it stood upside down. That way, the ketchup was always at the mouth of the bottle and easy to squeeze out.

So what if we pretended, as leaders, that we – our remote leadership, that is – are a product, just like a bottle of ketchup. And our employees are the customers using that product. Like Heinz, we would use empathy to understand our employees' experience of using our product, and we would find ways to make that experience better. We would carefully observe our employees' feelings, frustrations, workarounds, and, ultimately, their desires at work, and we'd design our leadership to give them the best experience.

IDEO Design Director Jane Fulton Suri describes the importance of 'thoughtless acts' in illuminating the opportunities for improving design that can only be caught by observation. Thoughtless acts are *subtle adaptations we make*, without thinking, to adapt to an imperfect environment. Two examples of 'thoughtless acts' that she gives are wrapping colored stickers around your keys to distinguish between look-alike keys or hanging your sunglasses from a shirtfront because they don't fit easily in a pocket.

Remote work, even with all of its benefits, is likely putting your employee in an imperfect environment. How observant are you about their subtle adaptations to cope with that environment and with you? What are their 'thoughtless acts', and how much are you thinking about how to eliminate those workarounds? I once worked for a woman who lost everything. Every time I gave her a copy of a document, I made a duplicate copy and kept it in a file drawer with her name on it because

I knew she would be back in a day or two asking for another copy. It was my thoughtless act to enable me to cope with her imperfect leadership (and we are *all* imperfect!).

Making this a reality calls for a new kind of leadership, a type of leadership we can think of as 'creative empathy leadership'. Creative empathy is about designing human-centric products. But what if we extended that and thought about leadership as a product? If creative empathy is the ability to understand how others experience the world and factor in their feelings when designing products, we can do the same when designing leadership. Incorporating empathy into each step of the design process helps designers create products and experiences that truly resonate with people – and the same process can work for leadership.

Let's imagine the employee is your customer and let's design a *leadership product* that fully observes and empathizes with its end user, a *leadership product* that cares and communicates with an understanding of how their employee experiences the world and what value it needs to deliver to them. Part One will help you empathize – this is where you will observe – and Part Two will help you design your leadership 'product' with the leadership behavior blueprints.

Your people are the job

When people ask me what I'll remember most about work, I will only remember one thing: the people.

Looking back over a career that has spanned almost 30 years, I only remember the people. I remember the first person who ever worked for me, who called herself by her nickname, 'Happy'. I thought I was doing her a favor by suggesting she use her real name, Hathaway, which I thought would make her seem more professional. She didn't pay attention to my advice, which was the right thing to do. Now she's an award-winning textile designer with work in major national magazines, produced under the label of her very appropriate and meaningful nickname.

I remember the people who quit working for me and all the months and even years I spent wondering what I had failed at as a leader to make them want to quit. Of course, it's not always the leader, but sometimes it definitely is.

I remember the people who have stuck with me and the people I have stuck with. I remember the managers I had when I became a working mom and how they kept pushing me to be the best I could be. One of them gave me air cover when I fell asleep at my desk in the first trimester then brought me a coffee. Another promoted me while I was on maternity leave.

I remember a friend I worked with in London who met me outside London Bridge tube station one morning after I'd had some bad news. I called my friend at his desk on the 13th floor of The Shard office building, looking up at the glass windows through tears, and asked him to come meet me outside. He took me for coffee and talked to me about his passion, basketball, to distract me while I pulled myself together. Basketball fans know the expression 'Ball is life'. My corollary for leadership is 'People are work'.

I will only ever remember the people.

There is a deeply moving scene in the opening episode of the Netflix series *The Crown* about care, duty, and work. King George VI sits during a break in a hunting outing to talk to a young Prince Philip about his marriage to Princess Elizabeth, the future Queen of England. He looks pensively at his son-in-law in the brume of a chilly morning and plainly states the one objective of his role as her spouse. It isn't titles. It isn't the dukedom. It is her. *SHE is the job*, he says. *She is the essence of your duty.* He must love her and protect her. There is no greater act of patriotism.

As a leader, *your people are the job*. You must love and protect the people who work for you. It's true, yes – love! The late management scholar Sigal Barsade, who taught me at the Yale

School of Management and later at the Wharton School, and her colleague, George Mason University Assistant Professor of Management Olivia 'Mandy' O'Neill, established in their research the importance of what they called 'companionate love' in the workplace. Companionate love is the love that we experience most often. They developed a methodology to measure this kind of love in the workplace and surveyed over 3,000 people in seven different industries, including pharmaceuticals and engineering. What their research showed was that where companionate love – defined as affection, caring, compassion, and tenderness – was expressed in the workplace, the employees in that organization had greater job satisfaction, greater commitment to their organization, and greater personal accountability.

Your remote employees must feel the authenticity of your care. They must feel your companionate love. And you can't do that authentically until you understand what kind of care they need and learn the techniques to deliver it – especially when they have different needs working remotely and you don't pass them every day inside a building. When we work this way, we have to be intentional about collecting information that can build real connections. Sigal Barsade was fond of saying that 'emotions are data', and we will use them as such in this book. Don't let them scare you off, and don't be fooled that we are in the realm of 'soft skills'. Nothing could be harder than truly understanding how people feel and caring about them.

Of course, empathetic leadership is important whether work is in person or remote, but the paradigm of being physically separated from the people who work for you makes empathy extra challenging for two reasons. The first is that empathy is more difficult to convey when two people are seldom face to face because you simply can't observe people and you have less information. And the second is that remote work is fraught with its own emotional patterns that are unique to working in physical separation from others. We will explore both challenges in this book and what you as a leader can – and should – do.

Part One:

REMOTE WORK'S FIVE EMOTIONAL PITFALLS

DIAGNOSTIC

Remote work Emotions and Mindset Questionnaire™ (EMQ) – Identifying the five emotional pitfalls of remote work

While your people might love the flexibility and independence of remote work, more challenging emotions are at play on some level all the time. A good leader understands these and is always on the lookout for them. Let's see if you are with this diagnostic tool.

The EMQ tool can be used in several different ways:

+ It was designed to be used in pairs, with a version of the questions for the remote employee and a version of the questions for the remote leader. Ideally you do this with one of your direct reports and compare notes to see if your perceptions of the remote employee's emotional experiences and mindsets align with how they really feel – or not.

+ You can also just use one version of the diagnostic depending on which version is most relevant to you – remote employee or remote leader. Sometimes you are both! The employee version will help you understand yourself better; the leader version will help you think more deeply about the people working for you.

Remote work Emotions and Mindset Questionnaire™ (EMQ)

VERSION FOR REMOTE EMPLOYEES

Rate each statement

0 = Never
1 = Rarely
2 = Sometimes
3 = Often
4 = Always

1. _____ My co-workers support me as much as I need.

2. _____ I have 1-to-1 conversations with my manager at least once per month.

3. _____ I feel content being at home for most of the day.

4. _____ I feel connected to what the rest of the employees in my company do.

5. _____ I get enough feedback about the work I do.

6. _____ If someone at work emails me in the evening, I will wait until the next day to respond.

7. _____ The work I do at my company is seen as important.

8. _____ On my work-from-home days, I take time to see friends in person or get outside.

9. _____ Others consider the work I do from home as *real* work.

10. _____ When people change roles or leave my company, I know about it.

11. _____ I feel motivated when I'm working from home.

12. _____ My manager cares about my well-being.

13. _____ I can be briefly offline without needing to explain why.

14. _____ I have a 'best friend' at work with whom I can share personal challenges.

15. _____ I am included in meeting invites relevant to my work.

Remote work Emotions and Mindset Questionnaire™ (EMQ)

VERSION FOR LEADERS of a remote employee

Rate each statement
0 = Never
1 = Rarely
2 = Sometimes
3 = Often
4 = Always

1. _____ I support my team as much as they need.

2. _____ I have monthly 1-to-1 conversations with my direct reports.

3. _____ My team seems content with their work-from-home arrangement.

4. _____ My team feels connected to what other company employees are doing.

5. _____ I give sufficient feedback about the work my team does.

6. _____ People in my team aren't expected to respond to work emails after hours.

7. _____ My team knows that the work they do at the company is seen as important.

8. _____ When my team works from home, I encourage them to take time to go offline for breaks.

9. _____ I feel that my remote employees deliver *real* work.

10. _____ When people change roles or leave the company, my team knows about it.

11. _____ My team can motivate themselves when they are working from home.

12. _____ I care about the well-being of each person in my team.

13. _____ Members of my team know they can be briefly offline without needing to explain why.

14. _____ Members of my team have a 'work best friend' with whom they can share personal challenges.

15. _____ Everyone in my team is included in meetings that matter to their work.

Remote work Emotions and Mindset Questionnaire™ (EMQ): Scoresheet

The scoresheet groups responses into the five emotional pitfalls of remote work: boredom, depression, guilt, paranoia, and loneliness. Each emotion is explained in detail in Chapters 2–6. Depending on your score, the emotion may be more or less present. See the scoring descriptions below.

Boredom	Depression	Guilt	Paranoia	Loneliness
Statement 3 ____	Statement 2 ____	Statement 6 ____	Statement 5 ____	Statement 1 ____
Statement 7 ____	Statement 12 ____	Statement 9 ____	Statement 10 ____	Statement 4 ____
Statement 11 ____	Statement 14 ____	Statement 13 ____	Statement 15 ____	Statement 8 ____
Total ____ Subtract your total from 12 and that's your score.	Total ____ Subtract your total from 12 and that's your score.	Total ____ Subtract your total from 12 and that's your score.	Total ____ Subtract your total from 12 and that's your score.	Total ____ Subtract your total from 12 and that's your score.

+ **A score of 9–12** indicates that that emotion is present and should be considered by the leader – see Part Two for leadership behavior blueprints, with discussion starters and empathy strategies organized around the Remote Leadership Wheel™. You can use this wheel to zero in on the emotional territory that needs the most attention from you as a leader, with actions to build connections to support your employee.

+ **A score of 5–8** indicates that that emotion is present and worth understanding in more detail – see Part One for more understanding of each emotion.

+ **A score of 4 or below** means that that emotion is only slightly present or not at all and likely not an issue.

Here's a watch out! **A gap of more than three points** between the leader response and the employee response on any of the emotions means that the leader perceptions are not aligned with the employee reality. It's valuable to know this information, which is why I suggest using the tool in pairs. Have an open conversation with each other about the gaps, and use Part Two to identify which supportive actions the leader can take to make things work – and feel – better.

Chapter 2

BOREDOM: HOW HOME OFFICE MONOTONY LEADS TO 'BOREOUT'

*L*ars is the manager of a team of software engineers in Germany. He worked from home only occasionally before the Covid-19 pandemic, but now it is more the rule than the exception. His company doesn't have strict mandates about coming in, so he and his team decide for themselves. The trouble is… Lars wants to go in but his team doesn't. It means Lars works from home more than he wants. He has never set up a proper home office because he thought working from home would be temporary. Some days he spends the entire day at his dining table and forgets to even stand up and move around.

When the weekend comes, Lars is desperate for a new environment. He needs to be out of the house. He and his wife and two kids do as much as they can outside of home during the weekends, but then, come Sunday night, they are all exhausted. There's been no time to rest. The place they used to rest and relax is now a place they don't want to be in when work stops. When Monday arrives, Lars dreads seeing more of his house, and he's craving a break from the same thing day after day.

The facts behind the feelings

Even before the Covid-19 pandemic, boredom at work was an issue. A 2016 study by Udemy revealed that over 51% of employees felt bored for more than half of their work week. And employees in the Millennial generation were twice as likely to feel bored at work compared to Baby Boomer executives. When asked why they would leave a company, employees said that 'boredom' was the cause 79% of the time.

In a 2021 workplace productivity survey of 1,000 UK employees, Capterra found that a fifth of respondents liked their employer *less* than before the Covid-19 pandemic. Boredom was the biggest reason they had fallen out of love: 42% said their job had become monotonous, boring or repetitive compared to before the pandemic. This was even a *greater* pain point than feeling that an employer's response to the pandemic was unsatisfactory, which was cited by 36% of respondents. And 25% said their job had lost its meaning.

Two Swiss business consultants, Peter Werder and Philippe Rothin, came up with the term 'boreout' in 2007. Boreout describes the sensation you have when your work has lost all meaning and you show up in body but not in heart or mind. Because feedback and the association we have with colleagues is so important to our feeling of meaning, it is easy to see how 'boreout' could quickly set in for a remote employee – those barometers of meaning are harder to tap into when everyone is confined to a Zoom screen.

And meaning itself is in a crisis: Reddit's niche forum on nihilism, subreddit r/nihilism, has grown from 31,000 members in 2019 to almost 130,000 at the time of writing. It's a burgeoning topic of conversation: nothing you do has any meaning or makes a difference in the world, so why do anything?

How boredom happens

According to industrial psychologists, boredom at work is considered a transient emotional state and is usually caused by three things: work tasks themselves, the work environment, or interactions of the employee with her task.

For the purpose of remote work, it's helpful to separate the causes into task related and environment related. Many remote employees will say they love their jobs but still struggle with boredom. Task-related causes of boredom come down to tasks that are repetitive, lack meaning, or are either too difficult or too easy for the employee. A person can also become bored when they don't have enough to do, or when workload is unpredictable. Such boredom at work can happen regardless of a person's remote work status, but when a person is remote, it can be harder to gauge if they are being underutilized.

Where boredom becomes problematic for remote employees is in relation to the work environment, especially the monotony of a person's home being the place they both live and work. It is impossible to get away from work when this is the case. The amount of time a person is at home begins to dull their interest in work – not because they don't like their work, but because they just can't stand the amount of time they spend in the same four walls.

I relate to Lars' story so much. During the pandemic, work-from-home boredom was intense, driven by the fact that nobody was allowed to go anywhere but their own house for sometimes months at a time. The 2020 Christmas and New Year holidays arrived without a company party, team dinner out, or even a visit with family. More days at home, days upon days.

I will never forget the intense familiarity I felt about my home. It felt like a jail cell. I live in one of the most densely populated cities in the US and our mayor ordered a 24-hour curfew in the worst early months of spring 2020. We could only leave to buy food or medicine, or walk our dog.

In a desperate need to put my head above the trench, I drove with my kids into Manhattan on Easter Monday, just to see what was happening there. We traversed Manhattan from bottom to top and back down again in about fifteen minutes, a journey that would usually take well over an hour in normal traffic. There was not a soul on the sidewalks, not a car on the street. I'm surprised a cop didn't stop me to ask why I was out. All the world was at home.

Colleen Crino has been remote in her role for five years, but travel helped make it bearable. Since the pandemic, that travel has slowed down significantly, and she agrees that being at her desk non-stop gets boring. She says that walking has become an antidote to that boredom: 'Now I take walks in the middle of the day. I never did that when I was in the office.'

Andrew Bolton, Managing Director of marketing software firm Knotch, acknowledged the inevitability of home feeling a bit mundane after a while when you work remote; it just goes with the territory. As Andrew says, 'You grow to accept your enclosure, like a goldfish.' Andrew has made it work over time by developing a work-from-home routine around a schedule that helps him maximize the value of working remotely: a morning walk, regular lunch time, and making dinner for the kids.

Another issue with non-office work environments is the degree to which we can be distracted by compulsions and interruptions. When we are distracted or interrupted, we lose focus on our work. When we repeatedly lose focus on work, we attribute that lack of focus to boredom. *I can't manage to get this task done, so it must be boring.* Boredom is usually accompanied by feelings of restlessness, irritability, and a desire to escape. It's a state of work that is the opposite of deep work or flow.

The Stanford economist Nicholas Bloom, who has studied remote work for decades, says that remote work has three enemies: the fridge, the TV, and the couch. But whether or not our home environment or work environment are more distracting is very dependent on individual circumstances, and dependent on individual self-awareness. Some people say home is the *only* place they can work without distractions, but not everyone feels that way.

Cristiana Pruteanu is a business operations consultant and self-described digital nomad who is based in Romania. She works with technology and digital businesses around the world and has worked remotely since 2009; she has also conducted training for Remote-how. She says that remote work became popular in Romania about a decade before the pandemic, with many people skilled as designers, developers, and technology professionals, jobs that are well-suited for remote work. For her personally, remote work has meant she could build a lifestyle that enabled her to travel and work at the same time, giving her a better quality of life.

Cristiana described a restless feeling that sometimes comes over her when she has been in the same workspace for too long. She knows exactly what to do because she's had years to perfect her remote work style. For her, being a digital nomad isn't just a way to see the world. She uses travel as a tool to counteract boredom and to support her motivation: '99% of the time I'm really motivated. Whenever I feel my motivation start to go down without an obvious reason, it's time for a new trip. Having done this for many years I know that every two or three months I need to plan a new trip. I already know when this is going to happen. I know myself very well.'

The first morning Cristiana is in a new place, she describes the feeling of being stimulated by a fresh work environment: 'My creativity is really boosted. This is part of the way I know I need to take a break from working at home, my creativity levels go down.'

Monotony of physical space is something every remote employee has to deal with – you aren't in an office building with multiple floors and communal spaces where you can hang out with colleagues. You don't have the change of scenery that comes with a commute. When you work in the same place that you eat and sleep, the monotony can feel intense.

In 2017, when I first became a fully remote employee, I started going to a WeWork in Manhattan one day a week. Because I worked for a multinational company, however, with my team a five-hour time difference ahead of me, my mornings started early, with calls from 7am. By the time there was a break in the action for me to commute to the WeWork, it hardly made sense to go. So after a few months of trying to make the trek out to a different workspace, I gave it up, and I probably suffered increased boredom because of it.

Boredom matters to the bottom line because of lost productivity from pronounced employee disengagement. Gallup calls employee disengagement 'the world's $7.8 trillion problem'. That's how much employee disengagement costs employers globally, amounting to 11% of global GDP. But boredom also has a human cost. People who experience boredom are more susceptible to depression, anxiety, anger, poor work performance, isolation, and loneliness.

The leader empathy scan: How to spot boredom

What complicates boredom is that it is hard to confess that we are going through it. The worry for many of us is that, if we feel bored, we must *be a bore*. So often, that means a remote employee will suffer boredom in silence, and it can be the gateway to more complicated problems.

When your employees are bored or have reached enough of a deep sense of boredom that you would consider it 'boreout', they will likely display these behaviors:

+ ask for different work to do;
+ ask why what they are doing is important;

+ allow scope creep (i.e., saying 'yes' to everything) to bring new content into their job;
+ take longer to deliver work – which you may at first see as laziness.

Leaders: Your next move

London Business School Professor of Organizational Behavior Dan Cable, author of *Alive at Work*, identified a system of thought in the brain that explains how we naturally seek to push the boundaries of what we know. We are innately wired to want to learn, to seek new information, and to delve into novel activities.

With the advent of industrialization, we intentionally removed novelty and meaning from work, the things that make us want to dive in every day. It was no longer the case that a pair of shoes was made by the same person who took the customer's measurements and completed the sale. Labor was divided and, with it, so was meaning. We intentionally suppressed curiosity from the work as something inefficient. For Henry Ford, 'curiosity' was a bug that he needed to take out of the manufacturing process. In modern companies, we are organized to work within a defined scope, 'staying in our lane', and curiosity and meaning are even discouraged in an effort to keep labor organized.

But the research points to how important meaning is in relation to boredom. When our work loses meaning, it just isn't interesting to us anymore. Meaning comes from understanding how one's work connects to the company's strategy, and how one's work makes something better for the customer, either internal or external. Simon Sinek would call this the 'why' of work – why does your employee log in everyday? Why is their work important to the company's purpose? What is *your employee's* purpose? *Their* why? Talk to them about it and maybe even get them to write it down. Codify purpose and meaning in how you run your team.

If you think boredom might be a factor for your employee, review 'Leadership behavior blueprint #1: Checking in' in Chapter 7. This blueprint will help you discuss boredom with your employee through discussion starters, and it will help you develop ways to create greater meaning in their work.

Chapter 3

DEPRESSION: HOW PERSONAL CRISES MAKE WORKING ALONE A SPECIAL CHALLENGE

*D*avid is a senior project manager for a mid-sized tech company that has always been remote-work-friendly. He's built a team of six other project managers and feels good about what he's been able to accomplish as a manager working remotely.

At home, though, things are different. Tensions between David and his wife were already bad before the Covid-19 pandemic and only got worse. Last month, she asked for a legal separation and David agreed. He moved out of the house and into a rental apartment nearby so he can see his two daughters, who are both in middle school. The girls aren't at an age where they can understand, and they both blame him for leaving home. His wife doesn't seem to even want him to see the girls, even though he doesn't think he's been a bad father. But he can tell she's been telling the girls the opposite, and they seem to be believing it.

David keeps pictures of his girls around his apartment and one on his desk, which he frequently looks at during Zoom meetings. He wonders if his marriage falling apart means that fatherhood will fall apart with it. There is nothing more important to him than being a good dad, but he doesn't know what to do. He

Googles for advice about the effect of divorce on children because he doesn't really want to bring it up with friends, many of whom are also friends with his wife. He doesn't want to bring it up with anyone at work; it's not really something you talk about over video anyway, even if he had someone to talk to. He spends a lot of time thinking about what went wrong, going back over the years they were together. How did he and his wife end up in such a bad place? None of it makes sense. He has never felt so alone.

The facts behind the feelings

The link between working from home and depression is inconclusive, mainly because depression itself has many varied root causes. Also, the experience of working from home is similarly varied, and everyone takes to it differently. A 2020 review across research from ten countries confirmed that impacts to mental health from working from home vary considerably and are dependent on both employer and personal factors: 'Working at home could have negative or positive impacts, depending on various systemic moderators such as: the demands of the home environment, level of organizational support, and social connections external to work.'

What is perhaps more consistent is remote work's association with mental health states that are linked to depression: loneliness, stress, and rumination. It could be reaching a state of Zoom fatigue, too much time in the same home office environment without a change of routine or scenery, or work hours overflowing into our personal lives, opening us up to the stress of work that seems to never end. The feelings of malaise we get from remote work has been referred to most often in the press of the last few years as the 'work from home blues'.

At the time of writing, depression continues to be inflated above pre-Covid-19 levels. In the UK's Office of National Statistics' *Opinion and Lifestyle Survey* in 2021, one in six adults (17%) experienced depression during the summer of 2021 versus 10% before the pandemic. Young people and women are more likely to experience depression. But for the most part, it is the pandemic driving these increases in depression, not remote work, though remote work removes some of the conditions that can alleviate depression, such as human contact.

How depression happens

The 'work from home blues' can surface in many different ways. Rumination is defined as a *deep or considered thought about something*, and it's a special hazard for people who work from home: there's just too much time alone to avoid it. When things aren't going well in our personal lives, it's really difficult to not think about life in a deep and considered way, because we're trying to work out solutions.

We can also ruminate about work. When a meeting doesn't go how we wanted it to go, we tend to go back over the things that were said and wish we had said them differently. When we are too quick to send an email and it blows up into a political reply-all-fest, we are hard on ourselves and play back all the possible ways we could have handled it other than via email. And sometimes nothing really goes wrong, but if we are prone to worst-case-scenario thinking, we run an event through our head over and over until we find something that doesn't sit right.

Rumination is harder to do when you're surrounded by other people. It requires a quiet and uninterrupted space, which is usually rare in an office. But at home, we have more of it. It takes a good deal of mental toughness to steer clear of rumination when there are no other factors to help interrupt our cycle of deep thought. At home, sometimes there is nothing to distract us apart from a pet.

When life takes a left turn, rumination and stress are dialed way up. The pandemic made us all feel raw and, as a leader, I often felt like I was in uncharted waters. Even as I write this, it's impossible for me to believe the threat of grave illness we all faced on a daily basis.

It began to feel out of place not to start my one-to-one meetings with an employee by asking how he or she was doing – and being prepared for whatever the answer would be. Some people were really not well. Sometimes they would want to talk about it, and sometimes they wouldn't. We all have a different level of comfort with sharing the things happening in our personal lives.

I'm somebody who really doesn't like to share much of her personal life, especially anything bad. And I don't like to pry. For me, the pandemic was a crash course in building connection using whatever means I could, but it started out with a focus on business, not personal. During the first few months of the pandemic, I recorded a three-minute video of myself every Sunday night and published it on Teams. The video was a look back/look ahead at the work we were doing: what happened last week that we should celebrate, and what do we have to look forward to this week. I wanted my team to see the light both at the back of the tunnel and ahead of it. This was early, when we thought Covid-19 would be over in a few months.

I soon learned to prioritize the personal if necessary. When the person I was talking to wasn't sure if their mother would be in or out of the hospital in the next few days, I made sure that conversation, in whatever shape it needed to take, had room to happen. The pandemic created what I think of now as *connection urgency* – when a house is on fire, you don't stand on the front lawn discussing how to groom the hedges.

I think it's important that we don't lose the learned habit of *connection urgency* that we picked up during the pandemic. Hopefully the issues we deal with in our lives in the years to come are much less scary than contracting a potentially lethal virus. Whatever our issues, though, connection urgency makes remote and hybrid employees feel the intentional presence of others, and it's the presence of others that makes rumination and blues a little less likely to take hold. Sometimes we really need someone to get in between us and our ruminating mind.

When I think back to the time before I worked remotely at all, reporting for work in a downtown Manhattan office building every day, *connection urgency* wasn't really called for. We were all together in one building, a steady ambient presence. We could leave our personal issues at home on the other end of our commutes. The office just wasn't the place for them.

I recall one July morning in 2009, a taxi driver named Abdul dropped me at the foot of the building I worked in. We had ridden together from Union Square and he had read my palm at stoplights on the way (that this is possible is one of the many things I love about New York City). He told me about my life and about me, and, I had to admit, he made a connection. He got a few things right that he couldn't have known just by looking at me.

When I got out of the taxi and turned to say goodbye, he pointed up at the office tower, and I'll never forget what he said: 'You aren't mean enough to work in a place like this.'

I shrugged apologetically and went into the building before being whisked to the 28th floor by a speedy elevator. Why did he think a person had to be mean to work there? What did the office building convey that was so replete with meanness? I didn't stop to ask him why he thought that, but there was something true about what he said that haunted me for a long time.

Only when the pandemic happened did I realize: we didn't need to connect when we were all physically together. We could take for granted that we were connected because, physically, we were in the same place. And while I was lucky to work with many great people, maybe it was possible for some walking the halls to be a little bit mean, as Abdul had said. Not only was connection not urgent, it could be fully snubbed altogether. It's a fallacy to convince ourselves that physical proximity creates emotional connection. It often doesn't.

As with something like boredom, we are unlikely to pipe up in a work conversation and say, 'Hey, I'm depressed'. It's a heavy word that has clinical associations, and it's a hard word to say out loud about ourselves. When I was diagnosed with breast cancer, I never could have said out loud that I felt depressed, but that is how I felt. I ruminated daily over my fears about surgery, radiation, cancer recurrence, and I even thought about death in ways I never had before.

The weeks after my breast cancer diagnosis were full of fear of the unknown, which I didn't share with very many people either inside or outside of work. At the start of my treatment, only my manager knew what was happening with me. Work was busy and I showed up, but mentally I was a million miles away. Even so, it felt like it would be scarier to stop working or take a step back, as that would make the diagnosis feel graver than it was.

Fear of the unknown was replaced with a deep depression when my radiation therapy started, two days after Christmas 2020. There was still no vaccine for Covid-19, so every day for a month I went alone to the hospital to have radiation beamed at my chest. After every appointment, winter weather permitting, I took a walk in Central Park, a few blocks from the hospital. In January, there is nothing much to admire in Central Park except for rocks. The wildlife has gone into hiding or flown away. The trees are bare. The blooms have blown off. The park looked like I felt, but I didn't know how to talk about how I felt. And work could be contained inside a computer with everyone thousands of miles away from me. The façade was easy to maintain.

After much reflection, I realized that the need to justify myself, to be constantly present online because I was not present in person, to grasp at cues of performance through emails and messages because I never saw anyone in person – all of those circumstances hyper-latched me to work, and it was unthinkable that I would step back from any of it, no matter what was happening in my personal life. Empathy could have helped me accept what was happening and feel supported, but I didn't let empathy in. I could conceal what was going on just by turning off the camera.

The leader empathy scan: How to spot depression

Sometimes, helping a colleague through a depressive period simply starts with letting them know you're available for them, with just asking 'How are you?' and encouraging an honest answer if you sense they are struggling. If someone shares with me that they have a medical appointment coming up, I put a reminder in Outlook so that that morning, I know to send them a text message to wish them good luck and let them know I'm thinking about them. But I never did that before the cancer. My personal experience has taught me that hearing from a leader, knowing they are thinking about you and supporting you through a difficult time, makes a lot of difference. Even if there's nothing they can do.

Aside from open conversation, there are some signs that your employee is coping with something challenging that are worth looking out for:

+ contributes less in meetings than in the past;
+ expresses worry or doubt on a regular basis;
+ seems reluctant to collaborate;
+ delivers work that is not up to their usual standard and misses deadlines.

Leaders: Your next move

None of us as managers can make depression, blues, or rumination go away. Sometimes our employees have hard things to cope with outside of work, and they will need the support of professionals, family, and friends. But the manager does have a role to play, too.

The manager is sometimes the most consistent presence in a person's life outside of immediate family, and, in my case, sometimes the manager knows things that even family doesn't know. My own manager was the first person I told about my cancer diagnosis, even before my husband. It wasn't my intention to do that, and in Chapter 4 I'll explain how it happened. Remote working was a factor.

Knowing our manager cares about what's happening to us goes a long way to giving us the support we need. Work is our connection to 'normal life' when the rest of life is not normal. We often even worry about our job security when life throws us a curve ball (I know I did – without work I would have no health insurance), and knowing our manager is in our corner and empathizes with what is happening to us takes some of that worry away.

If you think depression might be a factor for your employee, review 'Leadership behavior blueprint #2: Communicating with optimism' in Chapter 8. This blueprint will help you discuss what might be triggering depressive feelings for your employee through discussion starters. None of us are therapists and we won't likely solve what our employee is struggling through, but what is within our control is to make work a joyful place to spend time, either in person or online. Leadership behavior blueprint #2 will help you develop ways to create connections through joy at work.

Chapter 4

GUILT: HOW WE PUNISH OURSELVES AMID THE BLURRED BOUNDARIES OF HOME AND OFFICE

I gave birth to my first child in 2005 while I was early in my career in marketing at American Express. Around the same time, the company introduced an experiment involving work-from-home as a permanent assignment that employees could request to be part of called the Project Resource Team (PRT). The company's objective was mainly to reduce office space, but many employees understandably loved the flexibility.

I didn't choose to work from home as part of the PRT, even though it would have been the obvious choice as a new mother. To be very honest, I didn't want it to appear that I was on the 'mommy track', which I feared would stifle my career. Working from home with a kid wasn't really working in my mind, nor in the mind of everyone I knew. Nobody was doing it. Only 25% of US households even had broadband internet at the time. When I spoke to Susan Sobbott about the PRT for this book, she confirmed my experience: only about a dozen employees took advantage of it, all women, despite it being available to thousands.

The tension between office employees and home employees was something I felt palpably, and it persisted for more than a decade.

This 2017 comment on Glassdoor from a US employee at American Express illustrates the tension between those in the office and those at home: 'So many people would "work from home" on Friday that nothing got done. And if you emailed someone, there would be a "why are you bothering me" tone to the response.'

Oddly, my first encounter with remote work was to believe it couldn't work, and that it would be bad for my career to opt for it. Technology has undoubtedly changed my mind on the first belief, and my personal experience has proven me wrong on the second.

The facts behind the feelings

Not surprisingly, remote work carries a long legacy of guilt. Guilt is the tension between what you are *actually* doing and what people *think* you are doing. It's a feeling that you should be in the office, and the worry that office-bound employees will assume you are not pulling your weight, something psychologists call 'social loafing'. The irony about social loafing is that it happens when we're in groups, not when we're alone. But the perception is that loafing is rampant amongst remote employees working in solitude from their home offices. I assumed it myself when I was a new mother, and it's what kept me away from remote work.

In a recent survey of UK employees by LogMeIn, 46% of respondents felt guilty because of the *perception* that their working from home was not as productive as being in the office. And this was during a time when being in the office wasn't even possible because of Covid-19-induced office closures – the guilt persisted anyway.

According to the *New York Post*, a pandemic survey of 2,000 US employees revealed that fully two-thirds of employees worried about perceptions of their productivity at home enough to be concerned about losing their job, and one-third never took a break for lunch.

Add to this the negative backdrop of manager perceptions of productivity. In an early pandemic study of 1,200 managers by the Centre for Transformative Work Design in Australia, 60% of managers either believed remote employees were less productive than their in-office counterparts or were unsure if they were.

Neither managers' perceptions nor employees' fears align with reality. In Stanford economist Nicholas Bloom's 2011 remote work experiment, a cohort of call center employees for the Chinese travel agency Ctrip were sent to work from home for nine months to see what impact it would have on the business. Ctrip wanted to try this because, if it worked, they could reduce their real estate costs. The results of Bloom's study showed that the work-from-home cohort were 13% more productive than the in-office control group. The improvements were driven by more minutes worked due to fewer breaks and sick days and a higher performance per minute. Home employees were also more satisfied with work, with attrition among that population dropping 50%. What's especially interesting is that, when people *chose* to work from home after the experiment (versus being selected for the study), the effect of *choice* doubled the benefits of working from home. Keep this insight in mind when you read about autonomy in scheduling flexible work as part of 'Leadership behavior blueprint #3: Building trust' in Chapter 9.

Bloom maintains that remote work is a story in three acts: before, during, and after the Covid-19 pandemic. Before Covid-19, remote work was an anomaly and stigmatized as not being 'real work'. If you worked remotely before the pandemic, you will remember how people used air quotes whenever speaking the words 'work from home'. Pictures of people in hammocks or lying on beach blankets with laptops predominated the symbolism of remote working. And there are still leaders holding onto that old stigma: Elon Musk pronounced on Twitter that anyone at Tesla who wanted to work remote should 'pretend to work somewhere else'.

During Covid-19, remote work was not by choice, and it was being done under challenging circumstances. Matt Mullenweg, one of the founders of WordPress site builder Automattic, notably blogged at the start of the pandemic that Covid-19 was 'the remote work experiment nobody asked for'. Despite the fact that Automattic is a remote-first company with a workforce distributed across nearly 100 countries, Mullenweg acknowledges the importance of in-person meetups. Canceling them during the pandemic gave him cause for concern. What it means is that most of us haven't even experienced the 'right' kind of remote work – planned, intentional, and guided by employee choice, with a leadership that knows how to lead in this newly expanded way of working.

After Covid-19, Bloom predicts that the population of remote employees will see a fourfold increase from what it was before the pandemic. But with leaders like Musk deriding the legitimacy of work done at home, the stigma and guilt will no doubt persist.

How guilt happens

Profound gaps in trust between companies and workers is underneath guilt and the compensatory behaviors that go along with it. If you think you trust your workforce, read on. The data shows otherwise.

In a 2020 thread on Reddit, a remote employee admitted that he felt guilty if he wasn't 'in front of [his] laptop the entire day'. More than 200 commenters responded with a litany of reasons he should not feel guilty – *the company isn't worth it, you work long enough, it's not your problem if there isn't enough work to do, etc.* One commenter cautioned him to appear busy so he doesn't get replaced. Many of the commenters talked about the struggle to stay busy when they are able to get their work done for the day in less than the normal eight hours.

Ironically, because we are more productive at home, as Nick Bloom's research proved, our managers may not realize we have this extra time on our hands so won't know to adjust the scope of our work accordingly. This leads to dead time, and we either take the initiative to fill it or we don't, and we often feel guilty if we don't.

You're probably thinking that people should ask for more work and live with the consequences of guilt if they don't. What more often happens is that people get busy exploring other interests, both inside and outside the company. And outside interests that we have more time to invest in actually have the benefit of adding to our ideas and creativity and making us healthier and more productive at work. One person I interviewed said he uses the time he would have spent commuting to take long bike rides, and he feels better physically because he has more exercise. So maybe you can say there is reason to feel guilty about finishing early, but, on the other hand, employees are getting their work done and doing it faster, and some are taking better care of themselves in the process.

Aside from dead time, many employees will scramble to show up in as many ways as they know how, fearful of their job being at risk if they don't. This leads to a frenetic amount of overwork. It also means employees feel required to disclose more about their whereabouts or use of time, even personal time, so the boss knows they are still on task. This can be draining for both employees and managers.

In his guide to remote work, Darren Murph, Head of Remote at GitLab, identified that managing guilt and a 'toxic culture of envy' are disadvantages for employees working in hybrid-remote companies. Most companies today are hybrid-remote, defined as a company that has some employees in an office and some at home. In these cultures, remote workers are sometimes viewed as having 'finagled' a perk that office-based employees don't have. Remote workers may be expected to perform at a higher level because of this, need to justify their work arrangement if it's not available to all employees, or feel guilty about what their flexibility allows that others can't similarly enjoy.

Employee guilt about their work from home status is in some ways related to the phenomenon of 'presenteeism'. Presenteeism is when an employee shows up for their job, but, because of illness or a medical condition, they can't be fully productive. Studies in the *Journal of the American Medical Association* revealed that presenteeism during depression and pain drove three times greater productivity loss than just staying home with those conditions. As Covid-19 infections increased, many employees had to face the situation of their own presenteeism – logging in but doing far from their best work because their health wouldn't allow them, but also not taking the time they needed to get healthy either.

The UK's Office of National Statistics reported a 72% drop in working hours lost due to illness, from 3.1% in 1995 to 1.8% in 2020, and attribute part of that steep drop to the concurrent rise in remote work enabling people to work while they're sick. In the US, workers have additional motivation to work while sick, as there are currently no federal laws requiring an employer to give statutory paid sick leave. In many states, if an employee is sick, they either take leave without pay or use vacation time.

Micro-managing, time tracking, and electronic monitoring also all contribute to an employee feeling as if you assume they are not productive when working from home, thus triggering guilt. According to internet security and digital rights firm Top 10 VPN, global search demand for remote employee surveillance software spiked in the *very first month* of the pandemic, up 80% in March 2020 versus the same month in 2019. Search demand has nearly doubled every month since. I found this striking: employers' first reaction to the pandemic was to mistrust the very people – both employees and leaders

– who they were sending home in the interest of public health and saving lives.

GitLab's Darren Murph feels that surveillance is a copout, a leadership shortcut. He believes companies need to invest in tools that get work done, not watch people. He says that 'trust will win over surveillance every day'.

Because it conveys such acute suspicion, employee monitoring often backfires on employers. An article on the topic in *Behavioral Scientist* magazine explains it well: 'Monitoring employees can have benefits, but it can also decimate employee morale and, paradoxically, weaken ethical behavior. When companies monitor an employee's every move, they signal distrust, which can lead to employee disengagement. Disengaged employees are less productive; they can also introduce new risks to the organization as *people stop actively searching for the right thing to do* [italics mine] and focus instead on mere compliance.'

At its worst, guilt can be compounded when a remote worker feels that, now they are working from home, they need to be as available for demands from their family and friends as they are for demands from work. If I'm working from home, can't I just help out my friend who needs someone to walk their dog? If my wife has her hands full with young children and I'm in between conference calls, can't I help get lunch on the table? If my spouse works full time in an office, shouldn't I be the one to get the grocery shopping done and dinner on the table? We don't feel able to say no to the responsibilities that confront us at home, but this only makes our day more difficult and deepens our guilt on both sides of life – work and home. One person I interviewed eventually burned himself out trying to be everything to everyone while he was working from home, and it resulted in him resigning from his job.

If we try to do everything, we feel guilty for taking our eye off our emails. If we try to shut the door to our personal life during the workday, we feel like we've let the people at home down. I found this came up in a few interviews I did with younger workers, whose elderly parents and grandparents didn't understand that being at home didn't mean being available.

University of Arizona Professor of Management Allison Gabriel says that, when we work from home, guilt is 'multi-sourced': guilt from a supervisor, guilt from a family member, guilt from oneself, even guilt that we have a work arrangement others don't have. It can be a lot to carry around during the day, especially if we can't name it and have someone empathize with us.

It can even make us do or say unexpected things, things we would handle differently if we weren't in the continuous mode of needing to justify ourselves. One morning in September 2020, I was putting the finishing touches to a PowerPoint presentation I was due to share in a Microsoft Teams meeting with one of our company's executive vice presidents, a person I had had limited interactions with and wanted to make a good impression on. I almost ignored my phone when it started to vibrate on my desk with an incoming call, but then I figured I had few more minutes; I could take the call.

It was a radiologist who was calling to talk to me about the results of a stereotactic biopsy that had been performed on my right breast a few days earlier. What they had taken out of my breast in the biopsy was something called DCIS, or Ductal Carcinoma in Situ – an early stage of breast cancer. I would need to have surgery to remove it.

As the words 'cancer' and 'surgery' hung in the air, my Microsoft Teams widget started to blink. I had a message and opened it up. It was my manager asking if I was ready for our call, which was starting in only three minutes. *I need to go through with it*, I thought. *I can't just drop out, can I?*

My head was doing somersaults; my heart felt seized by confusion. *Are you ready?* he asked. I didn't feel like I could skip the call unless I had a really good excuse. A life-or-death excuse, actually. I moved a few fingers across my keyboard and typed *Doc just called and told me I have cancer. Please can you move the call?*

He wrote a few words of shock and encouragement back and repeatedly asked if I was okay. *Was I okay?* I just typed back: *I need to go offline*, and he encouraged me to do what I needed to do. Then I typed, through tears, *I don't know what to tell my kids,* then wished I hadn't. I was starting to react to the news, and I wanted to react alone.

It was only much later that I realized what had just happened: I had told my manager I had cancer before I told my husband, or mother, or children. My manager was the first to know. This was partly from shock, but partly from proximity. There was his instant message blinking in front of me while I was hanging up with the radiologist. And in some well-honed, but fully subconscious, instinct, after working remotely for so long, I felt like I had to have a good excuse to suddenly skip an important call while I was working from home.

I didn't know what I needed, but I needed a lot more from my leader than either he or I understood at that moment. Him being the first to know about my cancer diagnosis created a special need for care and empathy, but neither of us recognized it at the time.

The leader empathy scan: How to spot guilt

Despite reams of research about the productivity of home employees, when managers are asked, the majority assume productivity suffers at home. This makes employees work harder to prove themselves, risking burnout. And if a company is monitoring them, their disengagement will have pronounced impacts on their quality of work.

Born out of fear, guilt, and suspicion, employees will exhibit the following compensatory behaviors to try to convince you that they are worth their weight, especially when they work from home:

+ respond to emails outside of business hours and on vacation;
+ create unnecessary urgency and set unrealistic deadlines for projects they manage;
+ feel the need to explain how they are using their time, both work and personal;
+ request paid leave to do things like seeing a doctor or not use all their holiday allocation.

You can see how quickly these behaviors will lead to burnout, so it's important that leaders know how to get their remote employee off the hamster wheel of guilt.

Leaders: Your next move

To help alleviate their many-faceted feelings of guilt, employees must feel that you trust them until they prove otherwise, not the other way around. Too often with remote employees, leaders start with a negative balance in the trust account, but it's precisely trust that can help stamp out guilt.

If you think guilt might be a factor for your employee, review 'Leadership behavior blueprint #3: Building trust' in Chapter 9. This blueprint will help you discuss guilt with your employee through discussion starters, creating a greater environment of trust between you both.

Chapter 5

PARANOIA: HOW WE FEAR BEING 'OUT OF SIGHT, OUT OF MIND'

Kathy is a manager for a multinational sports equipment maker headquartered in the UK. Kathy finds out one day that a meeting has happened with everyone at her level, in her division, but strangely she wasn't invited. She assumes there must have been a reason. But what? Is an org change coming? Was she going to lose some of her remit or be removed from a high-profile project? She asks the organizer of the meeting if they can send her the recording or the presentation from the meeting, but they are slow to send it. Why don't they want to send it? Kathy sends a reminder. What was talked about? Kathy starts to feel angry about having a right to the information and not being able to get it. Leaving her out – or worse – feels like bad project management.

Kathy messages other people who she knows were in the meeting. She gets bits and pieces of detail from the meeting, but nobody is quite sure what her role is in the next steps. She starts to analyze everything she's said or done over the last several weeks, wondering if she made a mistake somewhere along the line that has led people to lose confidence in her. She is starting to convince herself that senior leaders have decided that having her in a meeting serves no purpose whatsoever. She reaches out to a colleague she knows well and decides to vent. The colleague reassures Kathy that it couldn't *have been that important, but they weren't invited either. They both commiserate. Someone finally sends Kathy the presentation, but she's so demoralized she hardly cares what she is looking at. It wasn't that important a meeting, no, but why wasn't Kathy invited? There's still no reason, until suddenly an email pops into her inbox from the organizer: 'Sooooooo sorry! I just realized you were left off. I was using an old distribution list!'*

The facts behind the feelings

Even as a write this chapter, our knowledge of the biases and disadvantages being faced by remote and hybrid employees is increasing substantially. I started this chapter believing that feeling left out just went with the territory of working remotely, and our unsettled attitudes towards it could most of the time be labeled as 'paranoia'. I didn't think there was that much evidence that we really *were* being left out. But in reality, there is quite a lot of evidence that says we are. And the more I delved into the dynamics of this emotion amongst remote workers, the more I realized I had encountered a perfect example of what Joseph Heller, the author of *Catch-22*, wrote about paranoia: 'Just because you're paranoid doesn't mean they aren't after you.'

What I write about in this chapter is paranoia, which is unsubstantiated harm, and it is different from true exclusion, an experience that results from biases against people who don't work in an office. If you are a leader who has little experience with remote work, both of these will likely look like paranoia to you.

Psychologists define paranoia as thinking and feeling that others mean to do you harm, even if there is little evidence to support that. You might feel as if you are imagining threats, sometimes called delusions. The type of paranoia I'm talking about with remote work is not the clinical type of psychosis called paranoid personality disorder. Paranoia of a non-clinical type is common; we all experience it now and then. The type of paranoia that surfaces with remote work is more about feeling that reputational harm will come to us because we are 'out of sight, out of mind'. We also legitimately suffer from what's called 'proximity bias' when we work remotely, and in those cases our paranoia is well founded and isn't paranoia at all; it's our understandable reaction to exclusion.

A 2017 study by US social scientists of 1,100 remote employees revealed that, on a range of interpersonal measures, remote employees don't feel as supported by their in-office colleagues. Amongst those in the survey who worked remotely some of the time:

+ 67% believed their colleagues didn't fight for them (59% for an in-office respondent);
+ 64% believed their colleagues made changes to projects without warning them (58% for an in-office respondent);
+ 41% believed their office-based co-employees were talking about them behind their back (31% for an in-office respondent);
+ 35% believed colleagues lobbied against them with others (26% for an in-office respondent).

So our perceptions are skewed more to the negative when we work remotely, but does this match reality? Stanford economist Nick Bloom's experiment of remote work at Chinese travel agency Ctrip found that employees who were sent home to work in the experiment were indeed promoted *less* than their in-office counterparts.

If your organization is or has embraced hybrid work as the best model for you going forward, these findings should be a shot across your bow. Hybrid work has many advantages and is a great model for flexing to what employees need, but proximity bias is a huge risk. According to an interview conducted by the Society for Human Resource Management with Jason Liem, founder and leadership coach at MINDTalk Coaching in Oslo, Norway, proximity bias is the 'antiquated assumption that people are more productive in an office environment than at home'. This assumption results in managers overvaluing the contributions of people in the office. Examples of this are remote workers being left out of meetings, better assignments going to in-office workers, and performance from in-office workers being more favorably evaluated.

Proximity bias is a double threat – not only does it lead to inequity between the people working remote and those in the office but also inequity between white workers and everyone else. We already know that white knowledge workers prefer working in the office more than women, people of color, and underrepresented groups. As the months and years go on and we likely settle into broadscale hybrid work, we may see our offices become exceptionally white and our remote populations become the most diverse, but also the most vulnerable to the effects of proximity bias. This risks sending diversity and inclusion efforts backwards by a long way if we don't manage hybrid work carefully.

Another flank of activity driving paranoia is the electronic monitoring of employees. While monitoring software can give us useful data about the way our work has changed, it also triggers huge fears amongst those in your workforce. In a recent study of 2,000 US employers and their employees by ExpressVPN and Pollfish, 78% of employers confirmed that they are using surveillance software to monitor their remote employees. What is alarming, however, is that employees found the prospect of surveillance, regardless of its data-collecting purpose, so disturbing that 48% of them were willing to take a *pay cut* in exchange for the chance to opt out of surveillance, with one in four saying they would take as much as a 25% pay cut! And employee surveillance across collaboration tools is only going to get more sophisticated. The software company Aware now sells an IM-monitoring tool that can enable a company to detect changes in mood, behavior, and sentiments – what they call 'authentic human signals' – based on an AI-driven analysis of messaging.

Even if employers relax surveillance, we are being watched (and judged) in other places, too. The Twitter handle Room Rater (@ratemyskyperoom) lets people rate the video call backgrounds of others and has over 400,000 followers at the time of writing.

Intel's Andy Grove famously told his employees 'only the paranoid survive'. He felt it was right to question the motives and intentions of other people's treatment of us. Paranoia in the workplace is what the researcher Roderick M. Kramer from the Stanford Graduate School of Business explains is a 'self-presentational' behavior. He has even termed it 'prudent paranoia' – looking out for oneself. Paranoia is a coping mechanism when our reputation feels at risk.

The January 2021 *New York Times* article 'Is Remote Work Making Us Paranoid' makes the point that 'many are feeling a spectrum of new anxieties about their interactions with colleagues', and some of those anxieties are paranoia. Small moments and gestures mean more than they should. Lines of communication might lapse because it's more difficult to keep connected when remote or through organizational changes. These dynamics create what one person in the article called a 'feedback break', and the result is that we overprocess and ruminate, unsure of where we stand. I've been through both organizational changes and remote work simultaneously, and I can confirm that the feedback break is real and connection is especially difficult to maintain.

How paranoia happens

As the data show, and characteristic of the definition of paranoia, an employee may convince themselves that others in the organization mean them reputational harm because the evidence to contradict that fact is less available when people are working remotely. A smile in an elevator, sharing a coffee in the office kitchen, bumping into someone in the parking lot and trading a word or two about a recent meeting – those interactions have ceased, and those are the kinds of interactions that blunt our fears of reputational harm. Feedback is broken.

But sometimes real exclusion is happening and an employee's reaction to it can look like paranoia, but it isn't. It's something a leader needs to pay attention to, as it is a warning sign that an action from the leader is needed to ensure the employee is included.

Paranoia as an emotional by-product of remote work was not something that had been well studied before the Covid-19 pandemic, and it is still an area that needs to be understood. During the pandemic, researchers developed the Pandemic Paranoia Scale and examined paranoid feelings emerging as a result of that worldwide event, why they happened, and what factors could help reduce them. Given that remote work was such a dominant work pattern during the pandemic, it's useful to understand how paranoia developed in parallel.

Researchers have found that stress is the most dominant factor driving paranoia. In a study of adults in five countries, some factors that protected people from feeling paranoid included maintaining a regular schedule, having trust in authorities, perceptions of low risk, or the belief that actions to prevent the spread of the disease would be effective.

Imagine those protective factors in a remote work context: regular work schedules were nearly impossible to maintain; we had less contact with our workplace authorities, including our direct managers; and perceptions of risk and how well we were 'flattening the curve' were subject to immense variations in data on the virus's spread. Add to that the unfortunate politicization of actions designed to prevent the spread and our lack of ability to be with others taking the same actions, meaning we lacked 'social proof' that what we were doing was the right thing.

In addition, during the pandemic, we were educated to understand that harm could come to us through other people. Any people – employees, friends, or family members. The mistaken belief that other people mean to do us harm is central to paranoid thinking, and we were literally conditioned to view others through that lens. So whether we wanted to be paranoid or not, we were being trained to be this way as a method of containing the virus.

Given that remote employees were already experiencing measurably more paranoid feelings about their co-employees before the pandemic, based on that 2017 study, one can only expect that, given the backdrop of the pandemic, our paranoia would increase. As Professor Kramer said in the *New York Times* article: 'Past research on the topic of organizational and social paranoia shows that working from home may exacerbate uncertainty about status. Remote work can contribute to feeling out of the loop, because you're missing the kinds of ad hoc conversations that tend to reassure us we're in good standing.'

The leader empathy scan: How to spot paranoia

Paranoia can make an employee voraciously hungry for praise and credit, the kind of feedback that helps confirm their standing. It's what Kramer called 'prudent paranoia'. Asking for praise and credit is how the employee seeks to calm their paranoia. They believe others mean to cause them reputational harm because all evidence to the contrary is minimal, and the inequities of proximity bias may indeed be diminishing their standing. They are strenuously trying to preserve their reputation, believing sometimes, and for valid reasons, that it is under threat.

To assess if you think your employee is feeling paranoid, be on the lookout for some of these behaviors:

+ expresses frequent doubts about self-worth and feelings of exclusion;
+ adopts tactics to conserve resources – possibly concealing information from you and others;
+ frequently asks about the whereabouts and meetings of other members of the team;
+ proposes or actively pursues interactions with more senior executives to increase proximity.

Leaders: Your next move

Research on paranoia from the University of Hamburg has found that it is closely linked to stress. What makes resolving paranoid feelings especially tricky is that adapting our beliefs to new information, which researchers hypothesized would help moderate paranoia, has no effect on the link between stress and paranoia. New information – evidence that a person's concerns are unfounded – doesn't seem to penetrate. Stress is a superhighway to paranoia, no off-ramps allowed.

This means that leaders need to treat paranoia as a symptom of stress. In the workplace, stress has a wide variety of triggers: unexpected events, low levels of communication, obscured cultural signals, confusion of strategy, or unclear expectations of outcomes. We know that all these conditions create a lack of clarity.

In the context of remote work, where cultural signals and informal interactions are limited, we can consider the emotional counterpoints to paranoia to be clarity and, related to clarity, equity. As a leader, the more clarity and equity you can bring to an employee's work experience, the more you will reduce the stress of uncertainty and potential exclusion.

If you think paranoia might be a factor for your employee, review 'Leadership behavior blueprint #4: Setting boundaries' in Chapter 10. This blueprint will help you discuss feelings of paranoia with your employee through discussion starters and develop ways to create greater clarity in what they do every day.

Chapter 6

LONELINESS: HOW REMOTE WORK CHALLENGES OUR HUMAN NEED FOR CONNECTION

Margot is a full-time remote employee, working as a contract project manager for companies in a range of industries. She lives in an apartment in a large city with her husband, two children, and a cat. Margot's husband Bill works late into the evenings sometimes, and her two children are active in school sports, often away from home all afternoon. Dinnertime is Margot's favorite time; she realizes that, on most weekdays, dinnertime is the only time she shares a room with other humans.

When Monday comes, and her youngest child is the last to leave, the click shut of the apartment door feels like a tomb closing. She shakes it off. Work pulls her in quickly and she tries to stay focused there. She made a resolution months ago to schedule at least one lunch per week with a friend so she has some human contact, but everyone is busy and it hasn't happened yet. Even though it would be good to have a break to go out, Margot dreads days when conference calls get cancelled because it means hours without even the company of other people on Zoom. One Wednesday afternoon just such a thing happens and she suddenly has three hours free after lunch. She tries to use the time for focused work but feels *restless. She's such a social person; other people tell her the quiet hours are great for deep work, but she's always struggled with the quiet. The silence gets pretty loud.*

The facts behind the feelings

While remote work gives employees more control of where and how they do their jobs, they may be paying for it with loneliness. Despite a remote employee's best efforts to generate human contact from those nearby, such as neighbors and family, it turns out that there is no replacement for direct contact with colleagues. A post-pandemic study on remote work revealed that loneliness from remote work actually *decreased* feelings of work-life balance. Counter to what we might think, if our direct contact with work colleagues is reduced, even if time with family and friends is increased, our work-life balance equation still won't add up.

Loneliness is one of the most common detractions of remote work. A recent survey of US employees by the American Psychiatric Association revealed that two-thirds of employees felt isolated or lonely some of the time and 17% did all the time. Worryingly, younger adults feel even more lonely: 73% of 18- to 44-year-olds were more likely to report feeling isolated or lonely working at home.

In the depths of the pandemic, UK hiring platform TotalJobs studied the same dynamic: almost half of UK employees felt lonely working from home (46%), and among younger employees aged 18–38 that figure ballooned to 74%.

The social media management company Buffer has been issuing a *State of Remote Work* report every year since 2018. Before, during, and after the Covid-19 pandemic, loneliness topped the list of complaints from the global sample of remote employee respondents. Despite that, in Buffer's latest 2022 survey, 97% of respondents say they would prefer to work remotely for the rest of their careers. So we know we're lonely, along with other challenges, but we're willing to put up with it in exchange for the flexibility.

Loneliness is an open conversation now that we've had several years of widespread remote work due to the Covid-19 pandemic. Rowena Hennigan, one of LinkedIn's top voices on the subject of remote work, author of the *Remote Work Digest*, and experienced author and instructor of remote work training in Europe, wrote this in one of her recent newsletters: 'I can feel disconnected and alone. Sometimes on the most hectic of days. There are sparse opportunities for real human connection. The quality of connection is lacking. Sometimes I also feel like I am the only one, alone in my role and responsibilities.'

How loneliness happens

Loneliness when working remote springs from the gap between the social contact we need and the social contact we get. It won't surprise you to know that we all need something different. For example, how lonely we feel working remotely depends very much on what researchers call social baseline theory. Social baseline theory (SBT) says that our baseline expectation of human activity is to expect social support and social contexts.

Some of us have higher baselines than others. So, when considering remote work, those of us with a lower baseline, or lower expectation of social support, may feel less lonely. Those of us with a higher baseline will feel lonelier. This makes even talking about loneliness tricky. When our colleague talks about how much they love the solitude, about being able to do deep work, we must think there is something wrong with us because we don't love it and are even sometimes overcome with restlessness.

We all have a gap between what we need and what we get. This gap contributes to emotional exhaustion. The exhaustion comes about because of a perceived resource gap – when we expect certain social support and resources but don't get them (or don't get them in person). To compensate for this, we take action to conserve resources and act with compensatory behaviors, like a person who has lost a limb and the remaining limbs need to get stronger.

Another important factor determining how much remote work will contribute to feelings of loneliness is the degree to which an employee prefers to separate work from home, or what researchers call 'segmentation preference'. If an employee has a high segmentation preference, it means they prefer to separate work from home to a high degree. They likely wouldn't be interested in any work-from-home arrangement. If they have a high segmentation preference, then working from home will be more dissatisfying than working in the office and drive greater feelings of loneliness.

The lesson is that *not all* of your employees will feel lonely. Those who will are likely those who have a high social baseline and high segmentation preferences.

We should shine a light on loneliness both because we care about the quality of work our employees do and because we care about our employees' overall well-being. Research has shown that loneliness has detrimental impacts on both health and work outcomes. In 2018, US Surgeon General Vivek Murthy declared that loneliness was a growing health epidemic. It was such an urgent health issue that he wrote a book about it – *Together: The Healing Power of Connection in a Sometimes Lonely World.* In his book, Dr. Murthy writes that loneliness contributes to increased stress and has been associated with a reduction in lifespan equal to smoking 15 cigarettes per day. At work, loneliness is linked to reduced quality of work, limited creativity, and reduced reasoning and decision-making.

Connections with friends – especially work friends – has a profound effect on work outcomes. A study from Gallup across 15 million employees around the world asked them if they had a 'best friend at work'. Only 30% of respondents said they did, but these were *seven times* more likely to be engaged in their jobs, were better at engaging customers, produced higher quality work, and were less likely to be injured. Those *without* a best friend at work had only a 1 in 12 chance of being engaged in their job.

Retired US Navy Commander and former Blue Angel Amy Tomlinson served several tours of duty as a naval aviator and grew up as the daughter of a naval aviator as well. She said that all her closest friends have come from the Navy community and have stayed friends for life. Reflecting on the importance of recent research on best friends at work, she agreed that such close friendships seemed to be a requirement to build the trust necessary to go into war together, fly off aircraft carriers, and trust each other with their lives. Friendship was undoubtedly a key ingredient to that trust and success. There's no doubt that someone with a strong sense of organizational culture and appreciation for connections at work has great prerequisites for the latest role she's taken on, developing virtual workspace employee experiences.

Even small interactions can help build strong friendships, and it matters less that you work together than that you share idle thoughts and feelings that are about more than work – which can be done in person, by email, or using remote technology.

For those liminal moments of interaction, John Riordan believes that the water cooler is not the answer. In his view, the water cooler is more widely known as the epicenter of gossip and negativity than for opportunistic encounters that lead to the next great idea. According to John, good remote managers are well structured in how they interact with the people they work with. They don't rely on bumping into someone to make a connection; they manage with intention, seeking out the people who will help them get 'out of their direct sphere' and learn something new or develop a new angle of collaboration. To rely on accidental meet-ups in an elevator doesn't look like a strategy.

Chris Flack, co-founder of the digital wellness organization UnPlug, acknowledges that remote work is fraught with loneliness, but the solution is to be thoughtful about returning to a healthy level of social regulation. During the pandemic, we learned that other people could inadvertently cause us harm by transmitting the airborne virus that causes Covid-19. So we stayed away from each other. Now, we need to return to healthier norms of social regulation, and that means flexing our social muscles, getting out to learn new things and meet new people, and meeting with colleagues when and where it suits the work to be done.

The leader empathy scan: How to spot loneliness

Part of the loneliness problem today is that we haven't learned how to restructure our interactions, relationships, and management with intent. We still rely on the serendipitous, ambient company of others to satisfy our feelings of loneliness – working in public spaces, for example, with a roomful of strangers doing their work in parallel with ours, but with whom we have no reason to interact. Is this really assuaging our feelings of loneliness?

As a manager, how do you know if your employee is suffering from remote work-induced loneliness? Here are a few of the signals:

+ has limited personal connections or friends in the company;
+ demonstrates counterproductive behavior, such as under preparing for meetings;
+ shows signs of stress through uncharacteristic actions or expressions;
+ has had a change at home that contributes to more loneliness, such as the departure of a roommate, child, or spouse, or the loss of a family member or pet.

Leaders: Your next move

Over and above watching for these signals, it's okay to ask someone if they are feeling lonely. It's not an easy topic to talk about so they may deflect, but they will likely be grateful to know you've opened the space to share, when and if they are ready. We can't fix loneliness per se, but we can empathize with it and lead with behaviors that can counterbalance the feeling of being alone. For example, a person who is *not* lonely is popular, befriended, sociable, close, and loved. In a word: they belong. For the purpose of supporting our employees, we can consider that an emotional counterpoint to loneliness is belonging.

If you think loneliness might be a factor for your employee, review 'Leadership behavior blueprint #5: Managing performance' in Chapter 11. This blueprint will help you discuss loneliness with your employee through discussion starters and give your employee a greater sense of belonging.

Part Two

THE FIVE REMOTE-READY LEADERSHIP BEHAVIOR BLUEPRINTS

THE REMOTE LEADERSHIP WHEEL™

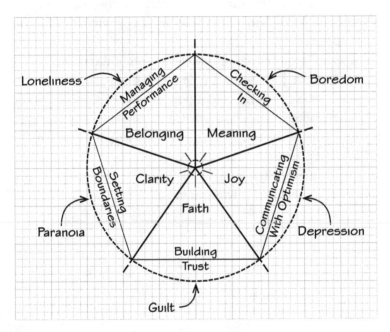

We talked in Part One about the emotional landscape of remote work and the dynamics of the five emotions that predominate. For each of them, there is an emotional counterpoint: meaning, joy, faith, clarity, and belonging. Part Two will give you practical steps on how to use these emotional counterpoints as tools to connect with your remote employee. But how do you do that? This is where the leadership behavior blueprints come into play.

How the leadership behavior blueprints are built

There are five leadership behavior blueprints for remote work: checking in, communicating with optimism, building trust, setting boundaries, and managing performance. You'll see how they work in the coming chapters.

Like an architectural blueprint, our leadership blueprints are each made up of five dimensions. When an architect uses a blueprint to build a structure, the dimensions indicate the specific size and measurement of each of the parts. In our blueprints, these dimensions will be your guides on how to build connections.

The five remote work emotions are often driven by factors that are external to work. The leadership behavior blueprints can't necessarily fix what's going on outside of work, but they will give leaders a list of compassionate actions they can take to empathize and build connection. This will ultimately make work feel better and your remote employee able to do their best work under their given circumstances because you have connected authentically with them where they are.

DIAGNOSTIC

Your leadership Remote-Ready Rating™ (3 Rs)

This diagnostic tool will help you assess how skilled you are at building connections *through compassionate action* as a remote leader, and where you most need to build your skills.

Rate each statement
0 = Never
1 = Rarely
2 = Sometimes
3 = Often
4 = Always

1. _____ I ask my team how they are when we meet one-to-one.

2. _____ I communicate several times per week with my entire organization.

3. _____ I ensure our team does something just for fun at least once per month.

4. _____ I tell my team how their work connects to the company's purpose.

5. _____ I am comfortable delegating difficult assignments.

6. _____ I discuss career development with members of my team at least once per month.

7. _____ I am able to encourage the quieter members of my team to engage.

8. _____ Employees in my team have mentors in the company.

9. _____ I talk to our customers at least once per month.

10. _____ I am able to decide my team's work schedule autonomously.

11. _____ I can laugh at myself.

12. _____ I empower my team to say 'no' to work if they don't have the capacity.

13. _____ I am able to be optimistic about change.

14. _____ I track the performance of each member of my team with measurable goals.

15. _____ My team knows how to advance work asynchronously (not everyone online at the same time).

Your leadership Remote-Ready Rating™ (3 Rs)

The scoresheet groups your responses around the five emotional counterpoints to remote work's emotional pitfalls: meaning, joy, faith, clarity, and belonging. Let's see how well your leadership style engenders these mindsets.

Meaning	Joy	Faith	Clarity	Belonging
Statement 1 ____	Statement 3 ____	Statement 5 ____	Statement 2 ____	Statement 4 ____
Statement 6 ____	Statement 11 ____	Statement 7 ____	Statement 12 ____	Statement 8 ____
Statement 9 ____	Statement 13 ____	Statement 10 ____	Statement 15 ____	Statement 14 ____
Rating ____ (Sum of responses)	Rating ____ (Sum of responses)	Rating ____ (Sum of responses)	Rating ____ (Sum of responses)	Rating ____ (Sum of responses)
Sum of ratings =		60 = Remote-ready perfection!		

In each grouping, evaluate your rating:

+ **A rating of 9 or above** means that you are strong at using this mindset to build connections. Well done!

+ **A rating of 6–8** indicates that you are competent at connecting using this mindset but there is more you can do – see Part Two for more guidance.

+ **A rating of 5 or below** indicates that you need to build your skills in using this mindset to build connections with your remote team. See Part Two for leadership behavior blueprints and discussion starters that can help.

Chapter 7

LEADERSHIP BEHAVIOR BLUEPRINT #1: CHECKING IN

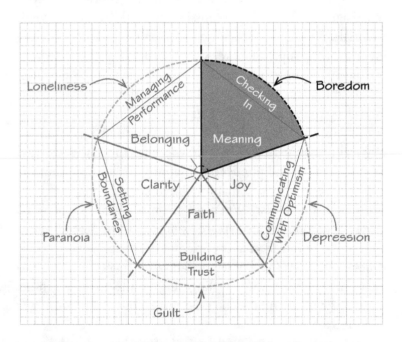

This leadership behavior blueprint is meant to support you in managing your team's feelings of BOREDOM by creating connections through MEANING.

There are many aspects of work that drive meaning, but you as the manager set the tone in your private one-to-one conversations as to how well such feelings can develop.

It's commonly accepted that the Covid-19 pandemic became a moment of reckoning about life and what matters, and this reckoning happened en masse. Not surprisingly, the labor market experienced such a high rate of resignations that the period directly after the pandemic began to be known as the Great Resignation. People realized that life is too short and while we're here we need to do things that mean something to us, or to other people. Meaning has become the biggest thing at stake.

It is only in your private one-to-one conversations that you can diagnose if meaning is missing at work, through signals and dialogue that are difficult or impossible when the meeting involves a group. Remote work wellness expert Rowena Hennigan doesn't mince words about the importance of checking in: 'The regular 1-to-1 conversation is the backbone of leadership in a remote context.'

Remote and hybrid work is characterized by a lack of physical proximity. Often people will refer to those accidental meetings, the serendipitous conversations, the liminal moments on the edge of real time that are the moments when we get to know each other best. When we share some of our personal selves. Your one-to-one replaces some of those serendipitous connection points by creating an intentional connection point. It doesn't need to be any less meaningful than bumping into each other in an elevator or lingering by the coffee machine. In fact, it has potential to be even more powerful because it is intentional.

At a work event in 2018 I met Celeste Helms, a colleague based in Arizona. She's a lawyer and works as part of our North American legal team. I work in global marketing, and, from a functional standpoint, we will seldom if ever work together. But when we met, probably at the coffee station or in line for the buffet, we just couldn't stop talking. She had two girls and I had two boys, and we compared notes on our kids as much as we reflected on the change we had seen at the company. We had a lot in common.

In a traditional work setting, she would have gone back to her office and me to mine and we might not have talked much again. Other colleagues in the office we work in would have played that role. But both of us were remote employees, her in Arizona and me in New Jersey. I reached out to her one day and suggested that we put time in the diary every month and just... shoot the breeze. Like we did that day at the event. She agreed, and we started what became a three-year (so far) cadence of regular calls on Teams in which we just talk about each other's lives. We talk about almost anything – stress, illness, ambitions, vacations, and dreams. It's intentional serendipity. The title of our recurring meeting invite is just 'Watercooler'.

Thanks to remote work we felt the *connection urgency* to make sure we kept in touch. Our relationship is intentional. We know the relationship would go away if we didn't maintain our schedule of calls, so we do.

In corporate jobs all over the world and in all different industries, I so often hear that people seldom have a one-to-one meeting with their manager, especially since the pandemic. That was a practice that seemed to quickly drop off the to-do list when we all went home. It made me wonder how intentional management practices had been when we were all in offices. Two McKinsey consultants, Tom Peters and Robert Waterman, in their best-selling 1982 management book *In Search of Excellence*, popularized the idea that, as a manager, you should take time occasionally to walk the 'front lines' and get to know your employees by casually walking around the office. This was called 'management by walking around'. I've recently wondered, now that there is nowhere to walk around, or at least less people to walk around with, do managers lose touch with how they should be checking in with their teams?

The bottom line is that, when one-to-ones don't happen, intention is missing. Maybe some managers still expect to pass members of their team in the office, be able to grab the occasional lunch or coffee, or catch up during other meetings. But the ability to sneak in 'catch-up' time in amongst other meetings is rare with remote work, in some cases gone altogether. We need to make a special effort to check in. When we don't, a 'managerial distance' is added to the physical distance, and remote and hybrid work really can't work.

Valentina Thörner, Head of Remote for an Estonia-based SaaS company and Remote Strategy Consultant, says she specifically asks in one-to-one calls about the rumor mill. She knows that people can be very creative living out their fears, and a leader needs to actively ask what is being talked about in the back channels. It's often full of emotional ghosts and goblins, and the leader's job is to turn on the light. A leader who only relies on group meetings to get to know people 'will never see the humans'.

Susan Sobbott makes a special point of calling people in her team after a group Zoom call, which takes extra time. Why? She wants to know what isn't being said, where a person's head is, what's truly on their mind that they won't bring up in a group setting. Susan takes Valentina's human insight even further: senior executives have such high demands on them to deliver business results that they can get stuck looking at their workforce as a 'block of capacity', mainly there for the purpose of executing on a business objective. 'We can forget there is a person standing in front of us', she explained. 'And now put that person inside a two-inch square on a screen and it dehumanizes them even more.'

Susan is emphatic that we're at a moment when the focus on the need for connection has to increase in any work environment, remote or not. But remote work exponentially increases the need for connection. Connection relates to demonstrating as a leader that you really do want to connect.

Leaders have to be proactive. It's obvious, but yet it's so hard. 'You've got to pick up the plug and plug it into the wall… it's not going to find its way there.'

Leaders, if it isn't clear yet, the ball is firmly in your court to make sure connections happen, and one-to-one time is part of your method for building them. You should encourage your remote and hybrid employees to also set up one-to-ones with their peers, even people they don't work directly with, like I did with my colleague in Arizona. My regular conversations with her give me a strong sense of belonging in the company and meaning to work, something we even talk about – sometimes explaining what you do to someone else who hears it with fresh ears illuminates so much meaning.

Drafting 'meaning'

As we understood in Chapter 2, one of the reasons we feel bored by our work is that we lose touch with what our work means. Helping your team find real meaning is a key antidote to boredom. In your one-to-one conversations, these are the dimensions that will help you focus on creating a sense of meaning.

Dimension #1: **Start with 'How are you?' and leave time for the answer.** This is the most important question you can ever ask someone who works for you. But more important than asking is actively listening to the answer. Control any temptation you might have to multitask. Close all other windows and silence your notifications. There is nothing that makes us feel *less* like opening up than when we are sharing something personal with someone and we can see their eyes darting across their screen and hear the soft tap-tap-tap of an email being composed while we talk. We shut down. Don't underestimate the opportunity for connection in the 'how are you?' question. Treat it with the utmost respect. Encourage your employee to answer it in any way they feel they need to.

Like Susan Sobbott's calls to members of her team – the call after the call – one of my former managers used to ask a great question: *How's your head?* I know he's not trying to be a psychotherapist. But the question signals to me that he wants me to talk openly about what's on my mind and he's ready to listen. Maybe it wouldn't work for everyone, but it's a question that makes sense to me. Often he is the only person to ask it, and it's the only moment in my week when I reflect on this question. How am I *really*? What's banging around in my head?

Sometimes an entire one-to-one will be about that single question, and you have to be okay with that. Follow up on the work stuff by email, but don't shortchange the check-in about the employee. Remember that empathy is defined as *the ability to understand and share the feelings of another person*. So in order to understand, you have to have the feelings explained to you, in the other person's own words, communicated in the other person's tone and manner.

You don't need to be hung up on using the camera when you have a one-to-one meeting, either. The camera is just a business tool; sometimes it's needed, sometimes it isn't. When I interviewed Scott Wharton, the GM of Logitech's video collaboration business, with global revenues of $1.5 billion, he told me that, when he does his one-to-one calls with his team, he often takes his phone and goes for a walk. I couldn't believe he of all people wouldn't use the camera. He explained that, when he talked to people he knew well and talked to frequently, the camera was superfluous. And there was something powerful about wandering on foot while having a conversation – it helped the conversation jump easily from topic to topic. And what he needed more often was the chance to leave his desk. Even more importantly, he knew that, with his one-to-one conversations, it was important to be in a place where he could minimize distractions and be a good listener, and his desk was not one of those places, with his email open and instant message notifications pinging his desktop.

Dimension #2: **Discuss purpose.** Does your employee feel like she is living her professional purpose in the work she does? Don't confuse performance targets with purpose. Targets by themselves have no meaning to us. That's because meaning is about being connected to something bigger than ourselves. Targets aren't bigger than us; we were hired to hit targets. So, effectively, targets *are* us. But meaning? That's bigger. Meaning – big meaning – can't be achieved alone. It's something that results from the collective action of many people working together. Ideally you should have a defined statement of purpose for your team, one that connects to the company's purpose in a simple and succinct way, and you can use that statement of purpose to check in on meaning during these conversations.

Leslie Carruthers is the founder and CEO of TheSearchGuru. com, an 18-year-old company whose employees have been distributed since day one. She wanted to be able to hire the best talent, wherever they were, and she herself had benefited from being tapped for a key assignment despite her location. From the start, she has thought about how to make a distributed team the best it can be.

One of the things she shared with me was her company's values, which include 'Ownership & Urgency', 'Figure It Out', and 'Respectful'. She says she hires for cultural fit and evaluates people in the team on whether or not they are displaying the values of the company. Even though everyone is separated by vast distances, from Ohio to Romania, it's obvious when someone isn't owning their work, or problem-solving with a sense of urgency, or showing respect to the team. Purpose and culture give meaning to each individual, but they also help Leslie evaluate the performance of her people. She said even her business partners have to fit her company's values or she knows the partnership won't work.

For Rowena Hennigan and the work she does on training and wellness for remote teams, meaning comes from developing shared values. These can come through team charters, team agreements – any document or even any visualization that helps a team understand what their values are. Leaders and teams should check in on these regularly and question how well the team is living their values through the work they do. Having a clear set of shared values also overlaps with psychological safety because it helps everyone in the team feel a part of something bigger that everyone agrees is worth protecting.

Rowena believes that when values manifest in tools, language, shorthand (such as BRB for 'be right back'), symbols, GIFs, and emojis, they create a values-based dialect that makes a team feel connected to each other, can enable highly personal expressions, and can even give cues and early warnings about emotional well-being and mental health.

Ilona Brannen, founder of the firm Slate Digital and host of the *Still Loading* podcast about leadership in the digital age, says you can't overcommunicate vision when working in a remote context. When we work remotely, the physical artifacts of vision and values – things like wall art, hallway graphics, logos, imagery, even the way a building is designed – that connect a company's vision and values to its workforce are much less visible. They need to be transmitted in statements of vision and purpose from leaders themselves on a much more regular basis. Sending physical company 'merch' to employees at home can also help bring a tangible asset from work into their home environment, and it's fun to receive things in the post!

Dimension #3: **Encourage and facilitate development.** Having some idea of the direction in which our careers and our life overall is headed is part of what gets us out of bed. When our work contributes to that direction, it has a special meaning. We know why we are doing it: to get somewhere we want to go. At the start of each fiscal year, the people reporting to me create development plans using a simple template that lists actions to achieve certain development milestones. For me, the most important box on the template is the one at the very bottom, where the person is meant to answer the question: 'What are your career aspirations?'

It's amazing how hard this question is for many of us to answer (including me). You won't have time to talk about a person's entire development plan in every one-to-one, but even if you just go back to the response in that box in your one-to-ones, it will help both of you check-in on how aligned a person's work is with their purpose. Does what they do seem like it's going to get them where they want to go? In answering a question like this, clearly mapped out career progressions in a company are vital or you will likely see your best people leave and your managers frustrated trying to keep them but unable to support their development.

Another important aspect of development is connected to broadening our cultural and geographic horizons, something else that gives life a larger meaning. Ricardo Fernandez, TEDx speaker and Managing Director in Spain for the German-based hospitality firm Limehome, told me that location was a key part of Limehome's talent attraction and retention strategy. Employees at Limehome are given the opportunity to take a 'Limecation', which enables them to work in a new location anywhere in Europe for a fixed period of time. He says that giving this kind of geographic variety and flexibility is the single best way to both attract and retain talent. A benefit like this helps keep Limehome out of salary wars with other employers, and the Limecation has become a part of the company's culture. At no extra cost to Limehome they can give employees comfortable, happy spaces to work in. In fact, they are seeing more companies using Limehomes as part of benefits packages to give their employees geographic flexibility.

Dimension #4: **Help your team effect positive change.** One of the reasons I love doing housework such as sweeping and glass cleaning so much is because they are two tasks at home where I can almost instantly see the results of my work. The floors look great, the tabletop gleams, and I did that! Seeing the results is what gives me satisfaction. At work, particularly when we are involved in projects with long timelines and complex dependencies, it can be really hard to see anything gleaming. In fact, it's easy to feel lost in a task, hanging up on one video call and almost instantly starting the next, like a monkey swinging from vine to vine to vine. What's even more difficult is that many of our meetings don't need to be meetings. Having too many outcome-less meetings can also make us feel disconnected from any meaningful results.

This is where communicating with optimism is so important, something we will review in Chapter 8. Remind them of the change you are after as a team, and communicate as often as you can about what they are doing that is moving the needle. Visualize the needle! There is a reason why fundraisers use thermometers to show the increasing amounts of money raised. Fundraising teams need to see that they are effecting change, and seeing money is hard when it is all whizzing around online. But when we see the level in a thermometer rising, we see ourselves making a change. How are you visualizing the positive impact of the change your team is driving? What will the change mean for your business and your customer? That question can have some very meaningful answers.

Dimension #5: **Don't forget that everything you do means something to a customer.** Talk to your team about the customer. What new things have we learned? What new initiatives or innovations have we launched or what evocative campaigns have we put into the world that have connected in a meaningful way with customers? Look at customer feedback together; if you don't have any, connect with the teams in your organization who do. I promise you that, in this day and age, every company has reams of it, and it definitely doesn't get looked at as much as it could. Keep a ticker-tape list of customer quotes, survey responses, Net Promoter Score comments, or product reviews on the side of your desk and mention a customer nugget or two when you are having your one-to-one. Even better, ask your employee to come to the one-to-one with their own customer nuggets. Ask them what they think it means. How should it define our next steps? How can we make life better for the customer?

I remember once spending two days interviewing customers at one of our trade show events in a round robin of short interviews, almost eight hours each day. It was the most concentrated amount of time I'd ever had with our customers. I found out over those two days how much they loved us. What's more, they needed us. They said things about our company and our products that even our best marketing copywriter wouldn't have been able to come up with. I will never forget one woman, who was widowed in middle age, telling me about the moment she had to take over her husband's business when he died. She had never handled finances before and the thought of doing so terrified her. Then she told me that our software made it possible for her to do something she never imagined she could do: handle her books. Not only was she able to successfully grow her late husband's business to make it stronger than ever, her confidence soared. She knew she would be okay. And our software had made her feel that way.

I left those two days of interviews feeling as if what I was doing was literally changing people's lives, making it possible for them to do what they never thought they could. There is so much meaning in that.

Here are five discussion starters for checking in:

1. How are you?
2. What has happened this week that you're excited about?
3. What did you learn from a customer this week?
4. What is one thing that has made you feel closer to your career aspirations this week?
5. What change are you part of right now and how do you feel about it?

Chapter 8

LEADERSHIP BEHAVIOR BLUEPRINT #2: COMMUNICATING WITH OPTIMISM

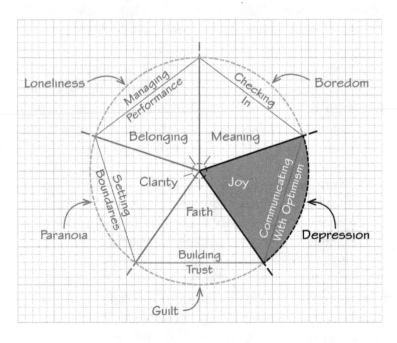

This leadership behavior blueprint is meant to support you in managing your team's feelings of DEPRESSION by creating connections through JOY (yes, joy!).

Optimism is hard for me. I once explained to my sister-in-law (an eternal optimist) that the way I make purchase decisions on Amazon is to sort by the one-star reviews. Her jaw dropped. When she asked me why, I said it was because I wanted to know how bad was bad. Before buying anything, I needed to decide if I could cope with what people were describing as the worst-case scenario.

It is probably because I have to work so hard at optimism that I appreciate it is such an important part of leadership. When a leader is optimistic, it conveys that success is a real possibility, maybe even inevitable, and that the challenges the team are facing can be overcome. It's sorting by the five-star reviews. It's asking the question: how good is good?

When a leader communicates with optimism, the team culture becomes anchored in hope and the excitement of expectation. Ken Chenault, in his podcast interview with Carmelo Anthony, said that 'the role of a leader is to define reality and give hope'. Having worked at one time in Ken's organization, I suppose it's no surprise, then, that I have a sign in my kids' bathroom that reads: 'Always believe that something wonderful is about to happen.' They are both teenage boys. When I hung it up, their eyes rolled. In truth, I bought it more as a reminder to myself than to them, so it's probably in the wrong bathroom!

Communicating with optimism matters when we work at a distance because of the negative self-talk we all suffer from. This is sometimes as loud as if it were being shouted through a megaphone when we are working in separation from others. We can feel dragged down by negative self-talk and a malaise can set in. Energy is low. In this blueprint, we will look at how communicating with optimism can help engender the emotional counterpoint to depression, which for the purpose of our blueprint is *joy*.

With joy, it's important that leaders don't feel they need to set the bar too high. Rowena Hennigan, who studies remote work and wellness, reminds us that some people just want to show up and get their work done and that's okay. The idea of joy in leadership is not that you are suddenly whirling through the Alps with your arms outstretched and a song in your heart. It's important we stay true to ourselves and not force a smile that isn't there. Joy can simply be something that makes you laugh and sharing it. Using modern tools to capture the sentiments of joy, happiness, and gratitude is important too. Hence the use of Loom video messages or audio messages are important ways to capture the real emotions associated with these feelings. When a leader is comfortable in their own skin, or even a 'work in progress' on the way to being comfortable, joy is a natural element of who they are as a leader.

One morning I posted a message on Teams to share a movie trailer with everyone in my organization's 'Taking a Break' chat channel. Anything goes in the 'Taking a Break' channel, and it's routinely where I find myself in fits of laughter, where joy happens in tiny, pleasurable increments. The movie trailer I shared was from the 2015 film *Vacation*, in which an adult Rusty Griswold, played by Ed Helms, decides to resurrect the Walley World pilgrimage with his own family. The movie is predictably campy, but my teenage son and I were beside ourselves with giggles. And so was someone in my team who works in Paris, who called the movie her 'guilty pleasure'. And someone else in Newcastle, England. And another person in London. And still another person in Los Angeles. It was a few minutes of shared joy that put a common smile on all our faces, despite the cultural and physical divides.

Drafting 'joy'

Communicating with optimism means you are able to point out where joy lies in the sometimes everyday drudgery of work. We are most alive when we are joyful. It is when we forget our worries and feel psychologically safe. Here are some ways to bring joy into your team's everyday work.

Dimension #1: **Be excited (even joyful) about change and what it means for your team.** Nobody loves change. But when you put on your white vest as Ed Harris does playing NASA's Lead Flight Director Gene Kranz in *Apollo 13* and it's time to abort your mission and get that rocket back to earth, you need to love the hell out of change. Missions change, and you still have to bring everybody home. Most people's natural instincts are to resist change; leadership is about being the one person in the room who will embrace it.

When change is coming, or has just come, spend time by yourself thinking about what it means for your team, for you, and for them individually. How might they be feeling about it? Scared? Excited? Ticked off? Start with how you think they will feel – empathize – before you enter the room with celebratory trumpets. Talk to people one-to-one. You will hear very little from a group.

When it is time for trumpets, think about what the change will bring that is positive. Where are the new opportunities? Where are the untapped possibilities? What ideas will this change inspire? How will it help the customer? In almost every change that happens in business, there are good answers to these questions, even in difficult changes like sunsetting a product, merging one business unit with another, or facing a challenger in the market. As a leader, it's your job to communicate what there is to be excited about, what the change means, and why optimism is warranted – but keep everyone's emotional states in mind as you do it and bring them with you.

Gabe Karp is the Managing Director for EMEA at the remote-first web agency 10up. He confessed to me that, eight months into the pandemic, stress and the intensity of deadlines made work miserable. Because of worldwide lockdowns, we couldn't do business in person, e-commerce had exploded, and websites had become new hives of activity, and that was driving a huge amount of work through 10up. A few projects were going over budget and risked client relationships and the health of the business. Everything felt too big and fast to control. During this time, Gabe became aware of how his emotions were projecting in calls, and how they were affecting the rest of the team. 'On Zoom, we're less guarded', he told me. 'In person we tend to filter ourselves a bit more.' He started working with a coach, who helped him show up projecting more positivity and control, which made a difference. But it started for him with recognizing that leading through Zoom meant leading with less of a filter, and the consequences are something that leaders have to be conscious of so pessimism doesn't creep in and bring down the joy of work.

Sometimes your team will just not want to be happy about a change. I learned this the hard way. Once, I had a person in my team who was having a hard time with a change. She wasn't helping herself or the team through change; she was actively fighting it. Her behavior even bordered on toxic because of what she talked about with others. I talked openly to her about how I felt, what I felt good about, and what I found challenging. She nodded her head to all the points I made and we genuinely seemed to be on the same page. I felt that I had been open with her about my own feelings, and hopefully I had encouraged her to be as open with hers. It seemed like she had been. Thirty minutes after our conversation she resigned.

One of the things I did wrong was to do most of the talking. I also confided my own feelings to her with probably a little too much candor, thinking that would help build a useful connection, and all it likely did was reinforce her desire to resist the change. The lesson for me was not to confuse commiseration with connection. Commiseration between a leader and employee doesn't build connection. When a leader commiserates with their employees, the effect it often has is to destabilize how the employee is feeling. If the leader is down, the team will be down. If the leader feels anxious, the team will feel anxious. So if you decide to commiserate, make sure you are commiserating about a thought, feeling, or action that you want your employee to emulate… because that's what they will often do.

Dimension #2: **Celebrate the wonder of both wins and losses.** A family with a little boy are neighbors of ours. Sometimes his soccer ball pops over the fence between our yards. He is not even five years old and quite shy, so every time this happens he is too timid to come into my garden to get it. I think he also feels that misfiring his ball into my yard is a no-no. One time, when I was returning his ball to him, I stooped down to his level and I said he was welcome to come into my garden anytime he wanted, but there was one rule. His eyes widened and I could imagine his little brain struggling to guess what that one rule could possibly be, and probably wondering if he were in trouble. Then I told him: the one rule was that, when he came to get his ball in my garden, he had to smell the flowers. He laughed. We both laughed.

I tell this story to remind you that your people worry a lot about making mistakes, and that worry can dampen their spirits when it really doesn't need to. There are wonders in making mistakes, even moments of joy. Things to discover. Holding onto wonder even in the face of failure is like stopping to smell the flowers. Your goal-oriented team is often too preoccupied to appreciate that there even *are* flowers. You need to be the forcing mechanism for that. Explain what it means. If it was a loss, what did they learn? If it was a win, of course point out to them how far they've come.

Dimension #3: **Make time for play.** Play is a critical component of feeling happy and joyful about our working lives. In fact, Daniel Cable, author and professor of organizational behavior at Oxford University, writes in his book *Alive at Work* that play and experimentation are most important when things seem negative and threatening. This is because play and curiosity stimulate what neuroscientists call our 'seeking systems', which help us achieve greater levels of creativity and collaborate more effectively.

During the pandemic, my team decided we would do the virtual happy hour one better: we hosted pub quizzes every Friday. Somebody was in charge of creating the quiz, and each week the PowerPoint show got more creative and hilarious. I'm sure I laughed hard enough to cry on more than one occasion. When we'd exhausted our pub quiz repertoire, we started playing online games like *Among Us*, where we each joined the game on our mobile phones, our avatars sparring in the mobile-based game, while on Microsoft Teams we chided each other continuously for gaffes in game strategy or bad luck. My kids caught me in an *Among Us* game with my team one afternoon and were incredulous: *This is your job?* They asked me. Yes, it definitely was.

Although we managed play using our virtual tools, I think play is one of the things that is great to prioritize for in-person meetings. Not only can it help motivate people to come into the office, in person is still the best way to enjoy each other's laughter and smiles. Even peripheral play lightens the mood. Susan Fitter Harris remembers the conferences and trainings she attended while an Administrator of Field Resources for the Local Initiatives Support Corporation, a non-profit community development organization. Susan recalls how the training team put toys in the middle of the conference table, things like fidget toys and Play Doh, which she believes helped everyone think better and have fun while they worked.

Also, be sure that, in an effort to streamline your team's work and save everyone time, you don't leave play time on the cutting room floor. Colleen Crino told me that remote work created a more meeting-heavy culture. To solve that, the company instituted a policy of 20- and 50-minute meetings, to give people a break in between calls. But Colleen missed those ten minutes because that was the play time. She wanted play more than she wanted a break: 'It cut out all the chit-chat and connection time, so nobody is following this policy.'

Shawn Kanungo is a sought-after corporate speaker on the topic of innovation. What he's observed time and again when he meets people from different organizations is how motivating it is to be creative, innovative, and learning new things. Shawn believes that 'play' even makes work a little bit more human.

Dimension #4: **Share each other's joy.** Part of building a culture of optimism and joy is being open to sharing our life experiences and how we feel about them. What is beautiful about sharing joy is that it is contagious! A study by the Harvard Medical School of 5,000 people over 20 years revealed that when a friend of ours is happy, that happiness can spread to others in their network by up to three degrees of separation, and the effect can last as long as a year!

The management scholar Sigal Barsade studied a phenomenon called 'emotional contagion' for many years. Her research showed that we can catch emotions from each other like viruses. And notably, our *leaders are more susceptible to catching emotions* from the people they lead than the other way around. Knowing this, it's worth developing a culture of joy in your organization because you yourself, as the leader, may enjoy a disproportionate benefit of all the happiness.

Lisette Sutherland is the founder and CEO of Collaboration Superpowers and author of *Work Together Anywhere.* The mission of her company is to help people work better together, no matter where they are. Part of her training emphasizes a model for being a 'Connected Leader'. In her many hours of training remote workers and leaders, she told me she notices a trend – low, or even negative, morale when people don't get the acknowledgment they need from their teams and managers for things like birthdays, milestones, and sales targets. When managers do nothing, it doesn't have a neutral effect; it actually does damage. 'How do we celebrate?' is the fifth component of her Connected Hybrid Team model. Joy matters.

Dimension #5: **Laugh at yourself first and foremost.** I was always one of those very serious kids. Things I thought were fun to do when I was in grade school included alphabetizing my library of books, or pretending to be a receptionist in a medical office. Keeping things in order was what gave me pleasure. Now that my job is about keeping things, projects, teams, etc. in good order, I've learned that I have to lighten up. But I'm also incredibly gullible. If you tell me the CEO wants me to send him a 96-slide PowerPoint on everything my team does, I will believe you and start working on it immediately.

One year, one of the people who worked for me sent an email on the morning of April 1st. The email said that I had signed off the creation of a 'kids' club' to help entertain and care for our customers' kids while our customers worked from home during the pandemic, with a huge budget and a big new team. I frankly couldn't believe what I was reading, but I didn't stop for a second to think what day it was. I messaged a few people frantically and ranted to my husband: 'I absolutely did not sign this off!' My practical joker let me swirl for a few hours and then reminded me what day it was. April Fool's. Earlier in my career I would have been irritated by all the energy I had wasted that morning reacting to a joke, but I just said to him, 'That was pretty good.' And it was.

Cathal Quinlan epitomizes the importance of making sure work is a good time – with humor, laughs, and fun. A former finance executive, Cathal left that field several years ago to start the podcast *Better @ Work*, aiming to help people make both work, and life, better. Cathal told me about his time managing teams. Keeping energy up was always highly important, like being a 'puppet master', he described. Holding people to account mattered, of course, but you had to give feedback in a way that was 'brain-friendly'. And if a meeting was dragging on, Cathal instituted a code word that everybody knew and was happy to deploy as needed – the code word was 'SUMO', and it meant 'Shut Up and Move On'. With a giggle, tangent over, the team could get on to the next thing. You can tell when you talk to Cathal that things need to be fun, first and foremost, and this was core to his leadership style. It also comes through loud and clear in his podcast. And the contagion is real: every time I listen to an episode of Cathal's podcast or talk to him, I feel joy. I wish I had met him when I was a kid, alphabetizing my library and playing receptionist. He would have set me straight!

Here are five discussion starters for communicating with optimism:

1. Tell me about a change you're going through and the opportunities it will give you.
2. What didn't work out this week and what did you discover?
3. What is one thing in our business that could use a change for the better?
4. Is there something that happened this week that the team should celebrate?
5. What is the most fun you've had this week – at work or outside of work?

LEADERSHIP BEHAVIOR BLUEPRINT #3: BUILDING TRUST

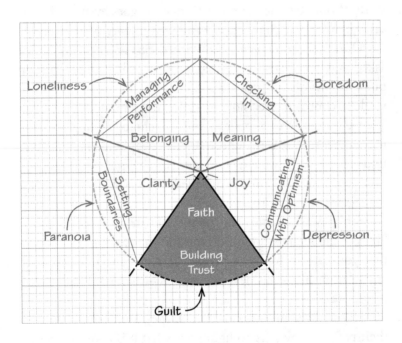

This leadership behavior blueprint is meant to support you in managing your team's feelings of GUILT by creating connections through FAITH.

I love Warren Buffett's book *The Snowball* on the business of life, so I'll borrow the metaphor: Trust is the clump of dirt that the snowball of leadership is packed around. Without trust, there is no leadership.

But getting to trust… that's anything but wintertime fun and games.

Thomas International, the global psychometric assessment solutions firm, created a pledge to communicate its trust in colleagues to determine their own work routine. The pledge says: 'We trust you to exercise good judgment in deciding whether you or your colleagues would benefit from meeting and working face to face some or all of the time. This will be left to individuals and their managers to agree, both acting in the spirit of our Remote Working Pledge.' It goes even further by saying: 'We value contribution and output over presenteeism.'

During an interview I did with their CEO, Sabby Gill, I asked him why he felt he needed to be so explicit about trust, to put those words on paper. He said that Thomas International made a conscious decision to call their remote work plan a 'pledge' rather than a 'policy', and the choice of words within it were because it was important that people in the company understood they weren't *just* words. The pledge is cultural – each colleague commits the pledge to each other, not just management committing to staff.

Sabby was unequivocal about the importance of trust: 'Trust is the single most important thing as a leader of a business that you can do for your people. If you don't have trust, in any relationship – business or personal – then you don't have a relationship.'

His message to leaders is that, if they don't have trust with their people, they have to figure out what it is about *them* that makes trust hard. Trust is too fundamental for any relationship. Go back to basics and ask yourself: what is it about that person that you don't trust – do you trust that they will do the right thing by you and them? If so, then what is the blocker? That you used to be able to see them and now you can't? Could that be a control thing that's your own issue rather than a violation of trust?

Sabby reminded me that we don't train leaders on how to trust; we just expect them to know how to do it. Trust is hard because it requires giving up control and being honest, with ourselves and with the other person. It requires taking risks that the other person deserves our trust and won't take advantage of us. And building trust is anything but formulaic. Sometimes we have nothing to go on but our instincts to tell us if trust is warranted. Let me tell you a story about my dad to illustrate.

In the spring of 1967, my mother brought my dad – then her college boyfriend – home to meet her parents. For many years, my grandmother had a woman working for her at home named Jeanette. Jeanette had had a string of bad relationships with men all her life and, as a result, she had a low opinion of all men. When my mother's older sister had brought her fiancé home to meet the family, despite how cordial I'm sure he was, Jeanette didn't like him. My mother remembers Jeanette remarking that he was 'too pretty'. When my grandmother remarried after my grandfather's death, her new husband gave Jeanette a raise on the day he moved in. Jeanette didn't trust him because he paid her money without knowing how well she worked. I'm guessing that she felt he was trying to buy her. So before my parents went home, my mother prepared my dad: *Jeanette just doesn't trust men. Don't worry if you can't win her over.*

When my parents arrived, Jeanette was waiting in the driveway with my grandparents to greet them. After meeting his future parents-in-law, my dad spotted Jeanette giving him a hard look. My dad at that age looked like Ron Howard in his *Happy Days* era: blond and fresh-faced, lanky and smiley. He walked over to her as casually as walking down the street and put his arm around her shoulder. He said, 'Jeannette? I hear you're a man hater.' And he gave her the warmest smile he had, and he meant it.

From that moment on, Jeanette loved my dad. The trust between Jeanette and my dad was instant. I think everyone in the family would agree with me that Jeanette trusted him more than anyone else. He was real with her, and that made her feel respected. And she paid him back with trust. My dad built trust like lightning set a tree on fire – so fast you couldn't even see it happen. An instant with him and the trust flame was lit. Because he said exactly what he meant, what nobody would say, and he meant every word.

The importance of building respect and trust as the leader of a remote team cannot be overstated. It's important for any kind of leadership, remote or otherwise, but when manager and employee cannot be physically together, trust creates a bond that doesn't need physical proximity to exist and helps build innumerable bridges. It's also the consistently key variable upon which successful remote and hybrid work arrangements stand. Being in person can do immeasurable good in building connections, but when face time is *more* important than work output, this is when employees say they don't feel trusted and everything else about work starts to decay – meaning, motivation, and productivity.

The web agency 10up's workforce is fully distributed around the world, and it was before the pandemic. In fact, when I ask Gabe Karp where they are headquartered, he explains to me that a remote-first company doesn't work like that. There are no headquarters. Gabe admits that they wouldn't even know what to do with a headquarters if they had one because employees are located in 25 countries and five continents. Literally everywhere. Trust is important for getting work done, but employees' hours are tracked for the purpose of client billing, and Gabe laments what this does to trust: 'Tracking time creates a feeling of a transactional relationship. There's an underlying tone where trust is hard to engender.'

When employees don't feel trusted, you will get their bare minimum, which is so much less than either of you deserve.

Thomas Cheney is a Senior Digital Transformation Manager for Lenovo. As with Gabe's team at 10up, members of Thomas's project team are distributed around the world. He credits his experience in the Marines for teaching him why a culture of selflessness and trust is the magic ingredient to performance: 'If you can demonstrate to your direct reports that you put their interests ahead of your own, they'll do anything for you.'

Finland is one of the world leaders in remote work, with 41% of the country's workforce working remotely and 91% saying they are happy with remote work, according to a recent survey by Statistics Finland. Trust is a big reason why remote work is successful there. According to a 2019 Eurobarometer survey, Finns trust their fellow citizens more than in any other country in Europe. Eero Vaara, a professor of organization and management and leader of the Future of Work research group at Helsinki's Aalto University School of Business, explains how trust figures in. It's thanks to a 'welfare model based on equality and financial security, alongside a culture of consensus-based decision making which promotes confidence in institutions'. He says that the Nordic countries have flatter organizational structures, less hierarchy, and greater pragmatism – all ingredients that make flexible working more feasible.

As I said earlier, I start with trust in the bank and then deduct as required. I make sure the person working for me knows that's the balance sheet. I will often openly say 'I trust you' early in the relationship, before the person has even given me a reason to.

But trust is a two-way street. Just because I trust them doesn't mean they are ready to trust me. My experience is that the higher up you go in an organization, the less you are trusted. I've struggled to get to the bottom of why this happens. My personal observation has been that the greater one's authority, the less vulnerability they demonstrate. People at the top don't feel especially safe being vulnerable in a work setting, and it's no wonder: we largely expect them to be unflappably in control. So they come to the front of the room, to the internal town hall, to the global email, with their work hat on. They are comfortable with that, and so are we. But we don't really ever know who they are, and it's impossible to be open and transparent with someone who is not open and transparent with us.

Valentina Thörner has been working remotely for more than ten years, and she believes that vulnerability is incredibly important to how she builds trust. She is openly gay and polyamorous and will refer to her girlfriends in conversations with colleagues. When she suffered the death of her father, she spoke freely about working through her grief with a therapist and has occasionally let her emotions show in meetings, shedding some tears. She sports a tiara in her video calls. Valentina has never bothered with the work hat. She is sure this is what makes people trust her, explaining: 'They know they won't be weirder than me. This builds a level of trust because I have trusted them with parts of my being.'

The obvious question I had for Valentina on the subject of vulnerability was how much sharing is too much? For Valentina, the question isn't so much what the leader is ready to share, but what employees are ready to hear. It's important that leaders start to put opportunities for sharing out there, starting with innocuous topics such as weekend plans, and waiting to see if the employee will share something at the same level. They may not want to share their private life, and that's perfectly okay, but it's up to the leaders to open the door and keep sharing at a level everyone feels comfortable reciprocating.

Chaya Mistry, founder and Director of the consultancy Humanly, is clear-eyed about the profound opportunity that trust presents to leaders and companies today. The pandemic was a moment when almost everyone on earth changed the way they lived. Arguably, we learned to live richer lives through more time spent closer to friends and family, more time reflecting on the things we care about most. Now is the moment that employers can tap into that richness, but only if they are thoughtful about the work experience they want their employees to have and willing to put policies in place that foster continued growth and autonomy.

Going all-in on trust isn't just table stakes, it's the whole table. To help us get there, let's dive deeper into leadership behavior blueprint #3's emotional connection tool: *faith*.

Drafting 'faith'

In her book *Joy at Work*, Marie Kondo explains the Pygmalion effect, in which performance rises or falls based on the level of expectations that are set for an employee. Applying the Pygmalion effect to tidiness, a person with a tidy desk is expected to have a greater capacity to produce quality work. Kondo tells the story of Lisa, a salesperson whose sales performance improved after she tidied her desk, for which her boss gave her high praise, boosting her confidence and continuing to improve her results. It all started when the people seeing Lisa's desk had faith that if Lisa could keep such a clean workspace, she must be a good salesperson. They didn't know Lisa's sales effectiveness yet but had faith it was there.

Faith is defined in the Merriam-Webster dictionary as a 'firm belief in something for which there is no proof'. It's even a braver form of trust than trust itself.

Dimension #1: **Champion autonomous scheduling as much as possible.** It's tempting for companies and their management to feel that, once flexibility is granted to employees, employees will be happy. But don't confuse flexibility with autonomy. Autonomy is when a company leaves it up to employees and their managers to decide what schedule works best for them.

The manager level at which autonomy is given is something companies should experiment with. Too far down and teams may miss the chance to collaborate with others whose manager has set up a different in-office day. This also makes purpose creation on in-person days, for example limiting virtual meetings, especially difficult.

Autonomous scheduling means that leaders have freedom to enable their employees to best balance their lives with their workload. A morning swim is worth ten meditation apps, as Colleen Crino would probably tell you. Because the CEO of her company emphasizes a culture of wellness and self-care across the organization, she doesn't think twice about blocking time from 9am–10am to get in a swim. She makes up the time in other ways, and she is that much more productive for the rest of the day because she's had some exercise and feels supported by the company to be healthy.

On the other hand, I spoke to a woman who is a 20-year veteran of her employer with a long track record of working successfully in a flexible schedule prior to the pandemic. The company recently asked its workers to return for 2–3 days per week, prescribing which days those should be. But this now presents her with a more restricted schedule than she had before, at least in terms of choosing her days in the office, and there really isn't a clear reason why.

University of Arizona Management Professor Allison Gabriel studies the 'science of recovery' at work. Recovery refers to recouping the personal resources that are lost after a hard day of work. Her research outlines how important psychological detachment is for recovery, but that's harder than ever to do when a person works remotely. It's up to supervisors to play an even bigger role in setting norms for recovery. Managers and their people should be able to craft the workday to suit both what work needs doing and what recovery is necessary.

Amy Blankson, the bestselling author of *The Future of Happiness* and a digital wellness expert, highlights the importance of how we use our recovery time. We all have sacred spaces and sacred times during the day – things that we do, or times we do them, that make us feel happier and more fulfilled, such as bringing a child to school or stopping work long enough to step outside and see the sunset. Managers know best what their team's sacred times and spaces are. When managers are given autonomy in scheduling flexible work, they can enable a schedule to make space for what is sacred in life. Autonomous scheduling becomes a powerful engagement tool.

Susan Sobbott recommends that leaders remember that, despite the fits and starts historically around remote work, the work world is in the midst of a huge transition. All the norms and best practices are still unfolding. Leaders should consider that, in terms of time in the office, there is no 'one-size-fits-all' solution. Going to a workplace involves time commuting, a professional wardrobe, a more fixed schedule, specific tools, and time set aside for in-person interactions both planned and unplanned. In Susan's view, not every day requires all those things. It doesn't make sense to ask people to be inefficient – i.e., to ask them to come to the office with all the related time-consuming activities to do that – and then not have a reason for them to be there. If your company chooses a hybrid model of work, with some days in the office and some at home, it's important to focus on making in-office days count.

Thomas International's CEO Sabby Gill decided that his company would not require people to return to the office. In fact, he's relaxed about where people work because flexibility is key in attracting top talent globally. He believes that diversity of surroundings encourages diversity of thought and innovation. You need to find the right balance that works for you and your teams, one size does not fit all. So whilst he encourages remote working, he also recognizes the importance of social interaction and physical engagement with his teams and brings together the leadership team on a fairly regular basis.

Dimension #2: **Prioritize care over inconvenience.** How many of us have gotten a message that says, 'My kid's nursery called and I need to go pick him up. I can't join the next three calls.' This event remained an outlier for working parents before Covid-19 because, for the most part, if a kid was sick, the parent just didn't come into work. But with Covid-19 it's created an off-again, on-again kind of day, where your employee may try to be engaged and join calls on mute, but you know in the background they have their hands full. As a manager it's tempting to be frustrated by this, and it's certainly possible to react that way. Work needs to get done.

I spoke to Anele Botha, who worked remotely from South Africa in a global team. She reflected what a difference it made for her when her line manager and colleagues treated her like a human being if she was interrupted by her 4-year-old daughter's needs. Nobody expressed any irritation or impatience if she needed more time to get something done. Everyone was sympathetic about her life beyond the video call screen and even asked how they could help. 'Beyond the hats we wear in the office, we are all human beings', she explained. When people at work understood this about her, she felt supported rather than stressed and guilty. Anele was radiant when she talked to me about receiving this level of support.

Feeling untrusted at a time of personal need can make an employee feel especially empty. My first remote experience was in 2009. I requested to work abroad for two weeks so I could stay with my toddler-age children when we took them for an extended visit to see my husband's family in Spain. I committed to equipping myself with internet access and a mobile with an international calling plan (both at my expense) so I could work from a distance. We rented an empty apartment, away from the family, for me to work in from the hours of 3pm to midnight every day, 9am to 6pm New York time. It would be a difficult schedule for me because I would be a full-time mom all morning and a full-time employee all evening.

At that time, remote work was a rarity, so the decision to let me work abroad for two weeks was escalated up several levels of management. I was given the green light, but it was a big ask. The day before I left, another manager who was soon taking over our team met with me in her office. She wanted to make clear that I would not work this way again, so I shouldn't get used to it. I left her office feeling like I had failed at working remotely before I had worked even one day that way. She and I had never worked together before and our relationship was just starting off. After that conversation, I felt like the door to trust with her had slammed shut.

For the next two weeks, I worked from Spain with the schedule we had agreed. Projects progressed on time, I attended meetings, made presentations via Skype, and even began to interview candidates for an open role on my team. I lived two lives during those weeks, the vacationing mom and the corporate marketing director. It was an exhausting privilege.

I felt successful in how I had managed the time and kept the work going, but I was never given any positive feedback. It felt like my request was something the company didn't want to say yes to but couldn't bring themselves to say no. So I was caught in the middle of their quandary, and my own feelings of guilt were the result.

The experience of carrying this guilt, and for working so hard to prove I was good for it and getting no acknowledgment of my effort, dramatically reduced my feelings of engagement and loyalty to an otherwise fine company where I had worked for close to a decade. The trust account had gone to below 0, and I felt empty at the thought of continuing to work for that company and that leader. When I returned from my time abroad, I resigned. There were other reasons, but my new leader expressing no faith in me from day one made the decision easier.

My experience is far from unique. When employees feel you don't trust them, not only do they disengage but they feel empty. Empty people can only do empty work. Leaders need to flip the trust ledger around, most especially with employees who work remote.

Dimension #3: **Develop a culture of psychological safety (and develop a culture).** Psychological safety has become a popular idea. What it is referring to is the ability for the members of a team to take risks, make mistakes, and not be punished for them. Equally, it is about creating an environment in which all ideas are welcome and no idea will be laughed at. When your team feels that safety, they will relax and be able to enjoy what they do. They will know you have faith that they will succeed in the bigger picture.

Maybe nothing causes more hand-wringing on the topic of remote work than culture. Won't we lose our culture if we aren't altogether in person? I think Leslie Carruthers' example in Chapter 7 of how she hires and evaluates employees on values and cultural fit is a prime example of how remote and distributed work doesn't need to mean the death knell of culture.

Similarly, Gabe Karp at the distributed web agency 10up is emphatic about the fact that we are blaming the wrong culprit – culture has suffered at companies in the last several years because of the pandemic, not because of remote work. Like all companies, 10up has suffered cultural atrophy in the last few years, but before the pandemic the company was fully remote and their culture was strong. Gabe knows it will go back to strength again.

As Gabe explained to me, 'The way you build culture in a remote setting is through intentionality.' 10up creates a culture where outreach is easy – Zoom anytime for a quick conversation, engender serendipity on Slack. Projects are organized in pods of small teams of 4–12 people that almost act as micro-communities, everyone focused on achieving success with one project.

Agnieszka Cisło, Head of Marketing for Froneri ice cream in Poland and Central Europe, thinks the reality of remote work is that many people in different generations may feel a certain lack of psychological safety precisely *because* of remote work. It takes a mature, self-assured person to feel comfortable with the uncertainty of remote work. Younger workers, early in their careers, will likely be full of anxiety about their futures and unsettled by the lack of career support they get when they work remote. Older workers, accustomed to the feeling of authority they used to derive from a floor full of occupied cubicles, may be battling feelings of insecurity or even see the lack of office-based workers as an affront to their position.

Trust requires honesty, but honesty requires trust. It can be a vicious cycle of never getting to the real deal. It's important to get the employee talking and you listening in an environment of psychological safety. And, most importantly, make sure they genuinely know you have heard them. When you show respect, they will repay it with trust. Like Jeanette and my dad.

Dimension #4: **Delegate and keep your distance.** The implicit message when you do this is that you have faith in a person's ability to deliver something without needing to be involved in the detail. It's the opposite of micro-managing. When we manage people remotely, it is very tempting to want to manage more closely because you feel you have less visibility of the work overall. My advice is to resist that urge and actually do the opposite. Put a challenging assignment in the hands of your employee, step back, and see what they do.

When I do this, I tell the person I'm putting them in the 'hot seat'. Nobody is ready for the hot seat if you ask them, but you need to do it anyway, then express your faith in them. Your faith will build their confidence, and ultimately you will get better, more creative work out of confident people. But if you never put them out there, confidence takes much longer to build, if it builds at all. This was the lesson in Marie Kondo's story about the Lisa the saleswoman. Her manager had faith in her to deliver results, so she did.

At first, the person I've put in that hot seat will want me to join every meeting with them and will copy me on every email, especially as we don't see each other in the office. It's their way of covering off every step of what's happening and ensuring I catch where they might be mishandling something. But I decline the meetings, and I gently remind them that they don't need me. I have faith that they will make the right decisions and, if they make the wrong decisions, I have faith that they will learn from the experience and be that much stronger in their skill sets and leadership. Throwing people in the deep end and stepping back is one of the best things you can do to demonstrate that you have faith in their skill and potential and give them a chance to build their own confidence in what they can do.

Dimension #5: **Attribute credit to your employees at senior levels.** Don't unintentionally hide your people, particularly the ones who are hybrid or remote. This will make them feel especially invisible. What do I mean by 'hide'? A leader who isn't close to what someone is doing and feels unsure how to represent it will have a tendency to gloss over, or ignore, the work they are doing in conversations with more senior leaders. Or there's limited time, and the work they understand less never makes the list of priority topics to be discussed. The problem might also be that the employee is perceived to be too junior, or senior executives don't know who they are yet or would be uncomfortable with the role they are playing in a project. There are lots of reasons why leaders hide people. Hierarchical companies are especially prone to this, and being a remote colleague puts an employee in an especially vulnerable position of being, or feeling, hidden.

Go out of your way to understand what your people are doing, especially those who are remote, and make sure that key stakeholders know who to credit good work to. I just told you to delegate and stand back, so how do you do this? It comes from making debriefs a regular occurrence (the one-to-one conversation can be used for this) and asking good questions. You can also put your people in meetings with you, or even in place of you, if appropriate. Have faith that your more junior people can handle themselves in a meeting with executives – too often I see a lack of tolerance for the unpolished imperfection of more junior people. Faith requires tolerance.

Here are five discussion starters for building trust:

1. What makes you feel most trusted at work and do you feel that you are?
2. Is there any accomplishment from this week you want to make sure I know?
3. Is there anything you think I should be highlighting to our executives?
4. How confident do you feel about X project? How can I help?
5. How can I be delegating more effectively to you?

Chapter 10

LEADERSHIP BEHAVIOR BLUEPRINT #4: SETTING BOUNDARIES

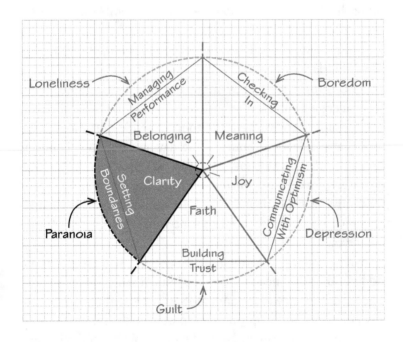

This leadership behavior blueprint is meant to support you in managing your team's feelings of PARANOIA by creating connections through CLARITY.

've had people working for me over the years who have all had moments of truth in their lives, and I always choose the person over the work. For example, a woman who once worked for me asked to work remotely while her father was terminally ill so she could spend more time with him. There's really only one answer to that question. But even in a difficult situation like that, it means setting boundaries and being clear about expectations. Paranoia can run both ways – you might find yourself as a leader of a remote worker and worrying whether or not they are really working. When that thought crosses your mind in the context of an employee caring for a terminally ill family member, it feels like you've misplaced your priorities, and it's pretty uncomfortable. So clear boundaries help. At the end of the day, you as a leader are still responsible for the work, too.

Before remote work became more common, the challenge with boundaries was about skirting corporate policy, and it was uncomfortable. In our more recent era of remote work, the challenge is about the policies skirting us. What I mean here is that, when we have the tools to work from home, our work is available at all hours of the day and night. This means we often feel that we should be, too. Research has shown that remote employees work longer hours because the time they spent commuting is now spent on work. It would be great if we used that time to get exercise or spend time with family, but that often isn't the case.

Sarah Hawley of Growmotely says that successful remote and hybrid leaders need to have the 'skill of self-inquiry'. Before large-scale remote work, boundaries were created for us – where to sit, our start and stop times, even our lunch and break times were all more prescribed. Now, the opportunity to designate a home and away workspace and manage one's own schedule can create an overwhelming level of freedom for both employees and their leaders.

If leaders are good at 'self-inquiry', they can identify what is important now versus what was important before, and sensible boundaries will be better established. They can be comfortable letting go and letting their employees make some of these decisions, and they can help guide on the priorities that remain. On the whole, Sarah says, we have to recondition ourselves from the way we used to work. Our formative years in school conditioned us to operate as a group, present and accounted for, in front of an authority figure. That is falling away – started by the Millennial generation and accelerated more broadly during the pandemic. Working adults expect a level of autonomy that was possibly unheard of even a decade ago. Leaders need to realize that the boundaries of their authority should be over the work, not the workers.

In my conversation with Laraine Miller, the President of Unilever's former tea business, ekaterra, she said she found it important to create boundaries. While the parent company created half-day Fridays in the summer, Laraine kept it going for her team all year long. At the peak of the pandemic, the company also set aside a two-hour block of time on Wednesday afternoons that were declared 'meeting free'. During those blocks of time, people were encouraged to do whatever they needed to do offline – exercise, see a friend, pick up their kids from school. Laraine and her team decided to continue the practice because it helped to 'bring in some sanity'.

She knows people will be tempted to overwork, and for her these institutionalized boundaries help her people find breaks, partly because everyone is finding the same break. It's become a part of her organizational culture, and everyone knows that you don't book anything on Wednesday or Friday afternoons. That said, she's grateful that Unilever's approach allowed business unit presidents like her to have full autonomy to try different schedule solutions, test and learn, and tweak to suit.

Drafting 'clarity'

Clarity is meant to help counteract feelings of paranoia, which we learned about in Chapter 5. In the context of the blueprint 'Setting boundaries', clarity helps your employee understand how they will collaborate with other teams, and it ensures they have all the information they need to do quality work. Boundaries help them collaborate on an even playing field with their colleagues and ensure work is equitable across your whole team – those in the office and those who are remote. Clarity in boundary-setting is about lifting the veil on unclear roles and responsibilities and the complexity of matrixed organizations. But even if you work as a solopreneur and lead a project team, clarity of roles has the same importance.

Dimension #1: **Enable your teams to work asynchronously.** According to remote.com, the definition of asynchronous work is 'the practice of working on a team that does not require all its members to be online simultaneously'. It's often praised by remote-first companies as being a key tactic in enabling both collaboration and flexibility. It requires sophisticated tools and a culture that enables and champions it, and its prominent reliance on documentation helps give minute-to-minute clarity on what work is in progress. Those in the know just call it 'a-sync'.

I have never worked for a remote-first company, so the first time I heard the term 'a-sync' was while doing research for this book. Once I knew what it was, I realized I had been doing it for five years! But because I didn't know what it was, and remote-first ways of working weren't part of my company's culture, I thought I was shirking my responsibilities if I worked odd hours.

For example, most of my distributed team is in the UK and would go offline when it was lunchtime where I was located. I used a few hours in the middle of the day to take my dog for a walk, exercise, or make myself lunch, then finished up my desk work in the evening when I didn't need to be online with anyone to do it. I never felt good about using the time this way because I had always been conditioned to think that work was 9–5. But with a-sync, it's not. The boundaries are different (and for me, better!).

I think of asynchronous work like a kind of trapeze act. Two trapeze artists on two different swings. One swings out while the other swings in, until one of them summersaults through the air and locks forearms with the trapeze artist on the other swing. That moment between the release and the catch is breathtaking. The leaping trapeze artist is supported by nothing, yet dives surely across the air between the two swings, confident she will land in safe hands.

It's probably going too far to say that co-creating a PowerPoint presentation with someone who is an eight-hour time difference away from you is like flying through the air between two swings, but the metaphor of having faith in the other person is the same. With a-sync, you know you can leave the work when it's time to go offline and the other person will pick it up where you left off.

If you don't have these tools already, implement cloud-based file sharing such as Sharepoint and instant message platforms such as Slack. I have used Microsoft Teams for the past five years and continue to marvel at how much easier asynchronous work is when we use it. For example, any meeting that I have in Outlook that day also shows up as an open thread in my chat in Teams, without me having to do anything. I accept meetings that happen for me at 3:00am simply because I know that, when I wake up, I will see the chat from the meeting, with comments from participants, and the recording and any documents shared in the meeting will be posted in that open thread. Over my morning coffee, I can attend meetings that happened while I was asleep, and I can follow up with the host or participants easily because Teams shows me who was in the meeting. The asynchronous documentation of work keeps projects moving whenever people can be online and gives clarity to project status.

If you are hosting a meeting, even if nobody asks you to record it, I would recommend you set 'record' to be automatic. A notification will appear at the start of the meeting so everyone is aware. You never know when you have a stakeholder in a time zone that doesn't overlap with yours, or someone double-booked in another meeting who wants to stay engaged in the topic but just can't join live with everyone else.

With a-sync and working across time zones, common courtesy often comes in handy. Thomas Cheney at Lenovo is based in the US and works with a colleague in China. He knows she is young with a young family, partly because he's heard them in the background during remote calls. When he's scheduling meetings, he makes an effort to fit them to her life context, neither too early nor too late, rather than his own. In the context of enabling asynchronous work, this also means relying on colleagues to complete work in between other commitments while headquarters or teams are offline in other parts of the world.

Valentina Thörner gives one note of caution on asynchronous work: it relies heavily on people who are good at writing and documentation. The fact that GitLab's Head of Remote Darren Murph holds a Guinness World Record for most prolific blogger, with more than 10 million words published across all media, is no accident. Darren is really good at a-sync style working and has spent years perfecting his approach to it. If we rely too much on optimizing our workplaces for asynchronous work, however, we risk alienating workers who don't have a Guinness World Record-level prolificacy or don't want to work this way, which compromises our diversity.

Dimension #2: **Practice 'communication patience'.** When we are seeking clarity, we want to know the answers to our questions right away. This 'hunt for clarity' creates a 24/7 culture in your team, when everyone becomes conditioned to check messages at any time of day or night in case a reply from them is expected. You don't want a team with a culture like this; you will quickly lose people to burnout.

I often tell my team in the UK that, if they see an email or IM message come from me after 6pm their time, I don't expect them to answer until the next day. In 2018, Microsoft introduced a flag in Outlook that appears at the top of a message if you are about to press send during the recipients non-working hours: 'You are sending this email outside of the recipient's working hours.' Next to the reminder is a button that lets you schedule the send. I don't use that schedule button nearly enough, but it's a habit I want to get into and the technology makes it so easy. Whether you use the tech or not, you definitely want to communicate to your teams that they are not expected to reply to messages outside of working hours.

Thomas Cheney's team is distributed around the world. He says that sometimes he'll end a call at midnight and find that someone has put in an invite for another call at 7:30am. He suggests that people who work across time zones should ideally have time blocks, like airline pilots, for a fixed duration of time when meetings can't be booked.

Like the trapeze artist, you have to have faith that the response will come when the time is appropriate for the other person. And you have to have the patience to wait for clarity, and teach your team to have patience by modeling the right behavior. Every once in a while there will be deadlines, but most of us are not heart surgeons or hostage negotiators. Everything that isn't one of those two things can wait. Make communication patience a part of your leadership style, build it into your culture, and it will soon become the norm – like ekaterra's Wednesday afternoons.

Dimension #3: **Overcommunicate. And then communicate again.** Organizational behavior was my favorite class in business school. When I was a student at the Yale School of Management, I took a course taught by the late professor Sigal Barsade called

Managing Organizations. On the last day, I remember her starting the class by walking around the room and saying the word 'communicate' over and over. Literally, over and over. She probably repeated the word 'communicate' one hundred times before she stopped. After about 30 repetitions of the word, all of us students looked at each other uncomfortably, wondering when this recitation was going to end. It kept going.

But here I am, 20 years later, and it's one of the lessons I remember best from business school. You need to communicate one hundred times more than you think you do. Often, I wonder if I should copy a person, or send an email, or have a quick conversation. The answer to all these questions is 'yes'. When in doubt, communicate. As long as you communicate in a professional way, you will never regret communicating, and you and your team will benefit from the clarity it brings.

Dimension #4: **Hold people accountable.** Whether you work on your own and are hiring someone half a world away or managing a distributed team, people who work for you or with you need the clarity of knowing what they are on the hook for. Claiming that they didn't know or understand that they were responsible for doing something is the get-out-of-jail-free card that gets played if you haven't explicitly documented who is accountable for what in any project you undertake as a remote team. Accountability needs to be documented and followed up on, on a regular basis.

When teams work less often in office settings, visible accountability (i.e., you literally see someone working on something) doesn't happen as often, or at all. So you need to be more explicit about milestones and decide what accountability looks like at each stage. Is it a section of analysis? Readout from customer interviews? Determine the tangible output that goes along with accountability and when it should be delivered. Make sure this is a central part of your documentation process, especially if you do more asynchronous work.

Dimension #5: **Teach your team to say 'no' or at least 'not right now'.** When our paranoia overcomes us and we worry about being 'out of sight, out of mind', every request to do something or be part of something calls to us like a siren song. It's tempting to say 'yes' to everything, but we really can't. Quickly we are triple booked throughout the day while multi-tasking in the one meeting we decided to attend. Many remote employees fall into the 'yes' trap because it makes them feel more present, visible, and less likely to be forgotten. You need to give your team the permission and confidence to say 'no' and reassure them that they won't be forgotten if they do. Remind them to be clear about their goals and what they need to deliver. If they fill up their days with meetings, they risk underperforming.

Your team needs your 'muscle' to keep the volume of work in check, but be careful about setting up policies that can have unintended consequences. Virang Patel, who worked at the time in product development at Citigroup, told me that in a typical day he would receive 400 emails and would be in as many as ten meetings. Being at home and handling meetings from his desk enabled him to toggle between meetings and email, so he managed to stay on top of things better throughout the day than if he had been in person in an office. In an effort to curb the fatigue of non-stop video meetings during the Covid-19 pandemic, Citibank's CEO, Jane Fraser, instituted a 'Zoom-free Fridays' policy. But for Virang, this meant that all his meetings that used to be on Friday got shifted to Thursday. Thursday became a nightmare. By saying 'no' to Friday meetings, Citibank's CEO actually created a bottleneck of meetings on the day before.

Here are five discussion starters to help you with setting boundaries:

1. Is your current schedule clearly aligned to your goals?
2. Is there any project you're working on that needs to be communicated more across the company?

3. Can work keep going with other members of the team while you're offline? How can we improve that?
4. What is one thing you can stop doing?
5. Who is accountable to you and are they delivering?

Chapter 11

LEADERSHIP BEHAVIOR BLUEPRINT #5: MANAGING PERFORMANCE

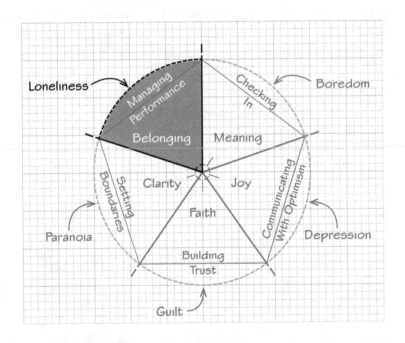

This leadership blueprint is meant to support you in managing your team's feelings of LONELINESS by creating connections through BELONGING.

Managing performance is what every leader is worried about with remote work. Are people really working? Was somebody offline for the last two hours and you wonder why? Do you find yourself checking the little status bubble next to their name – green or pale yellow, and for how long?

But there is another side to performance management besides just getting things done. Did you ever participate in a sport as a school kid and feel the exhilaration of dunking a basket, discovering you were the first to the wall at a swim meet, finishing a long-distance race, sliding into home plate, acing a serve, or scoring a goal? The same can be said of academic achievements, extracurricular milestones, or any moment in time when you could proudly say 'I did it!' What is so important about those moments is how our friends and family react – sharing our excitement, showing their pride in us. The belonging we feel from achieving something as part of a team or in the eyes of others watching us is one of life's best moments.

In the context of 'Leadership behavior blueprint #5: Managing performance', belonging comes from that pleasurable feeling of accomplishing something and how it makes us feel, especially when we do it as part of a team, squad, or group. A big part of belonging is the experience of just being seen. When we work remotely, we are rarely literally seen. But when we accomplish something, we stand out, and we also fit in.

At the start of her TED Talk, Susan David, the South African-born psychologist and bestselling author of *Emotional Agility*, greets the audience with a traditional Zulu expression for 'Hello': *Sawubona*. *Sawubona* literally means 'I see you', and especially all that you represent – your values, your passions, your experiences, and even your future. I especially like what you are meant to say in reply: *Shiboka*, which means 'I exist for you'.

The heart of performance is just about getting stuff done. Existing for each other, seeing each other's results.

Drafting 'belonging'

Proponents of remote work will say that managing performance is not about where and when the work gets done; it's about measuring outputs. So in theory, it should be easier to manage performance when a person is working remotely because you only have to think about one thing – the outputs. Here are ways to measure performance in a way that helps your employee feel that their outputs are seen, giving them a greater sense of belonging at the same time.

Dimension #1: **Highlight achievements and hearsay.** When you see the work your people do, you see them. If you struggle to remember everything they're doing, don't worry. Managers, especially of large teams, have a lot going on. Take even ten minutes before the call to prep just a little, jot down a few notes. Scan through emails and IMs if you need a reminder. Check your diary – were you in any project meetings together? What did they do in that meeting and who attended? There will definitely be one thing you want to mention.

Something else that helps promote belonging is to share with your employee what other people in the organization, especially leaders, have remarked to you about what your employee is doing. Even if it's constructive (e.g., 'It would be great to understand the ROI better'), it shows that not only do you see your employee, but other people do, too, and they care enough to give feedback on that person's work.

Taking a step like this can especially help with belonging in cultures where remote work is a strange departure from what everyone is used to. Jennifer Sakaguchi, a communications professional for Rio Tinto, based in Tokyo, explained to me that, culturally, Japanese offices are all about face time. Before the Covid-19 pandemic, it would be expected that you stay in the office until your manager went home, even if you had nothing to do. Face time mattered a great deal to how one was viewed in the company, even more than productivity itself.

Now that remote work is more prevalent in Japan, Jennifer doesn't see it going away. She sets up more meetings than she strictly needs so she can see people, and she tries to travel as much as she can.

An important part of achievement is managing workload. Ask regularly if a person has enough work to do. This can be difficult to notice, especially when you don't work side by side in an office building. And if you see their output slowing down, you might be tempted to think they aren't putting in the hours, when what is really happening is that their pipeline of work has just slowed down, or they are finishing work faster. There's an easy fix for that – more work! Be sure to assess this before you jump to the conclusion that their productivity has dropped. Aside from the obvious importance of productivity, we need a robust pipeline of work to feel important to the team, to feel we belong.

Dimension #2: **Measure everything – what gets measured gets done.** We can thank management guru Peter Drucker for that adage. A manager I once worked for said something similar: 'Numbers focus the mind.' If I tell you to go out and get some exercise, you might walk around the block for five minutes and be done. Every day your exercise routine might look a little different, so different that you wouldn't really be able to accurately compare your improvement from day to day. But if I tell you to do 50 push-ups every day, you'll count them and know exactly what you've done from day to day. And the even better part of knowing your number is that, when tomorrow comes around, you will be filled with ambition to beat the number you did the day before. Measurement is profoundly motivating.

I talked to a manager who was frustrated that one of the people he was managing just wasn't getting their work done. He told me about how this person left early and arrived late (this was in an era of mostly working in the office). This employee never seemed to be at his desk when he was in the office. The manager was exasperated trying to figure out where he was all day and what he was doing, but the manager was worrying about the wrong thing.

When I probed to find out what the root cause of the problem was, I learned that the employee in question didn't have any measurable goals. They were working on the creation of a new program that was all white space. The manager had directed this employee to launch the program, but that was simply a matter of sending out an email announcing that the program was available. Then what?

We talked about setting monthly targets, and I advised this manager to meet weekly with the employee. Document the targets with empty boxes for each month that the employee was expected to fill in with performance data. In weekly one-to-ones, the conversation about performance should be about the numbers in that chart, not where and when the work is getting done. If they are increasing, work is getting done. And the great thing about seeing data points about performance is that there is no question of success (or struggle). It gives an employee a great boost of confidence to see data rising based on things they are doing.

It feels too basic to even say it here, but new managers and managers new to remote work get deeply distracted by the 'where is my employee?' worry, so much so that they forget they haven't put a measurement framework in place to discuss performance. When you have a measurement framework, you can talk about what's getting measured because what's getting measured is what you want done.

Dimension #3: **Talk about slippage before it becomes an ongoing trend.** To follow on from the scenario in the last dimension, leaders of remote employees can struggle with the need to bring up poor performance. The best thing you can do for someone who isn't performing well is to open up a dialogue about it. They need to know, and they need to know you know. And you're not being a pushover to proceed with empathy.

Try to start by assuming positive intent and seeing how much you can understand about the employee's life at that moment. You don't know what challenges and personal burdens your employee has on their shoulders. They could be significant. And yet, the slippage may be entirely due to blockers at work. Start the conversation trying to understand all the blockers.

Should you ask about schedule and time spent on work as one of the potential blockers? Absolutely bring this up if you think the person is sabotaging their success by letting distractions at home take over their day. But the way to handle this conversation is not with a tone of 'gotcha!' Like the scenario above, use measurement frameworks to keep things factual and focused on outcomes.

In my team, each person creates five performance goals at the start of the fiscal year. They list the key milestones for each goal and an estimated time to achieve those through the course of the year, along with a few (less is definitely more) quantitative metrics that can be used to determine success. We've all probably heard of the acronym SMART – it refers to goals that are Specific, Measurable, Achievable, Realistic, and Timely. I find that SMART is a good framework to develop goals because you have all the important criteria covered.

Setting SMART goals and measuring everything makes slippage easier to spot. If you can spot it, you can talk about it. I suggest that using a word like 'slippage' helps because of the psychological safety it creates – it's an easier way to talk about what could be characterized as falling down on the job. And the term suggests that it's only a momentary lapse that can be recovered from.

Don't have too much anxiety about knowing whether or not a person is doing what they are supposed to. Gabe Karp at 10up says he has zero concerns about productivity. You don't have to hunt for poor performance, it quickly becomes obvious when you see multiple rounds of feedback or projects drag on. His advice is to look for the obvious cues – they are there.

Dimension #4: **Connect work output to team, department, and company vision and purpose.** You've no doubt heard the adage: 'There's no "I" in "Team".' Well, there's also no 'I' in 'Success'. Successes that we achieve by ourselves lack that certain emotional electricity of bursting across the finish line after a relay race and seeing the exhausted faces of the people who ran the relay with you. My team once relaunched a global website, which required round-the-clock monitoring of the site's stability as elements of the code migrated from the old code base to the new one.

I'll never forget the instant messages of excitement and camaraderie when, at close to 4 o'clock in the morning, the site was declared fully migrated and stable, job done. How deflating would that moment have felt if we had had nobody to share it with, just us and our exhaustion alone? And we celebrated despite our distance – Dublin, Atlanta, New York, and Newcastle.

As a leader, creating teams or squads that have a singular focus on achieving a goal together is a way to ensure that not only is work properly resourced, but everyone gets there together. Squad membership is especially important for remote work in large multinationals. Thomas Cheney was a Pricing Planning Manager on the development of the IBM ThinkPad back in the early 1990s. The ThinkPad was developed by a team that included employees from Scotland, Australia, the US, and Japan. The core design team was in Japan and part of what Thomas thinks of now as an 'island of excellence'. Their design expertise was acknowledged and appreciated as being the best, and Japan the best place for design to be executed, even though the rest of the team were located in other geographies. Distributing the team was the path to success.

Thomas credits the international team of people with the success of developing the ThinkPad because they were collaborative and willing to build off each other's strengths. Each member of the team, partly because of cultural nuances, approached problem-solving differently, and Tom feels this helped bring the best thinking to the table. What Tom remembers about that launch is the tight cohesion of that distributed team and achieving success together, despite the distance. And this was in the 1990s, long before cloud computing and the communication and collaboration tools we have today.

Collaboration expert Lisette Sutherland advises leaders and teams to take advantage of all the tools and technology that help us to 'work out loud': making our work visible so that others know what we are doing, even while we are remote. Lisette emphasizes that this is not the same thing as monitoring. Being able to 'work out loud' creates an environment of parallel productivity, in which teams can more easily shift into moments of collaboration, and it becomes more obvious how everyone's work interconnects.

For example, the software Sococo enables workers to work in a virtual office, to sit side-by-side online, and to 'see' what each other is working on. It's also possible for employees to update their status in Microsoft Teams or Slack to state what they are working on. This lets colleagues drop in to help or ask a question if it's related to what's currently on an employee's virtual desk.

Dimension #5: **Encourage mentorship from elsewhere in the company.** For several years in one role, I was mentored by one of our company's senior executives, who ran an area of the business that I did not work in. She mentored me about career decisions and how best to identify and fill skill gaps, but she also asked me the kinds of questions about my current work that only a leader with 'low context' would ask. Describing my work to her, and what we were achieving, allowed me to practice communicating with senior leaders and learn how to use plain language, dispense with acronyms, and paint a picture of why our achievements mattered for the customer and the company in terms that she, as a senior leader, could understand.

Sometimes we don't realize how accomplished we are until we talk about it out loud with someone who has fresh eyes. They help us reflect on accomplishments by connecting what we've done to what the company needs in new ways. They energize us with their wonder at learning something new. And this infusion of new thought, energy, and wonder is a shot in the motivational arm when you've spent a long day on video calls, in the trenches with colleagues who are more familiar with what we do. Also, choosing a mentor *inside* the company is more helpful for belonging for obvious reasons than choosing someone from outside.

Here are five discussion starters for managing performance:

1. What goal is at risk, and do you know why?
2. What goal has already been accomplished, and what new one can we replace it with?
3. How will you measure X? [where 'X' is any task or project]
4. Who helped you achieve that milestone and how?
5. What type of mentor at our company would be most helpful to you?

CONCLUSION

We've proven that, for many jobs, we can decouple our workforce from our workplace and still get our work done. Even better, we've discovered that, when we do this, we can be more present for our families and reduce the stress and expense of commuting that used to be a routine for five days out of every seven. And we understand that remote work isn't just about logging in from a different desk; it's about adjusting to an asynchronous rhythm, communicating differently with our leaders and organizations, protecting the boundary between work life and home life, and becoming more intentional about our relationships with our colleagues and teams. This gives companies so many more options to balance employee quality of life with how and where work gets done, whether through a fully remote or hybrid remote model.

At its core, remote leadership is about connecting with your teams using the tools of empathy. The Remote Leadership Wheel™ is your guide to decode the emotions and mindsets that your remote employees hold, in varying degrees, for much of the time. With the chapters on the five emotional pitfalls in Part One, you now have a lexicon to talk about the many possible answers to the all-important question: 'How are you?' I hope you see yourself or your employees in some of those scenarios and you feel seen and understood as you read that section. There's nothing wrong with you if you feel any of these things; it's what those of us who work remotely are all feeling sometimes. Have faith that you are in good company.

As I wrote this book, I was constantly reflecting on how tempting it is in professional settings to veer away from emotions

– it's almost a rule. But management scholar Sigal Barsade often said that *emotions are data*. They give us important information. She emphasized that they are not, as is often assumed, in conflict with rational thought. They *are* rational thought. Emotions and mindsets give us a frequency, a channel on the interpersonal walkie-talkie, across which to connect with each other. So in addition to reminding you that emotions are data, I would go one further and say that *emotions are tools*. I don't mean manipulative tools, of course; I mean connective tools. They help us empathize with each other and share common, human experiences. Design Thinking relies on empathy and careful observation to deeply understand what customers need and to design products that will deliver a great value and experience. Our leadership is our product, and empathy is our path to a great experience for the people who work for us.

I learned my own lesson about shutting down connections when I was diagnosed with cancer. Remote work made that easy. Compartmentalization through a Zoom screen, at the time, seemed like a good way to handle what was happening to me, but it ended up cutting off my access to the community of work friends and colleagues who could have empathized with me and supported me. If you are a leader, remember how easy it is for your people to hide their struggles, traumas, and even everyday frustrations.

Sharing in general is hard, but it is often the only way for us to feel connected to each other. It's up to you as a leader to open the door and signal that you are present and listening. Why should you? Because Sigal Barsade also said that employees don't leave their humanity at the door. Whether we want to accept it or not, a human being is on the other side of the screen. And the more of that human you can connect with, the better their work will be.

GitLab's Darren Murph told me that leaders need to know that 'empathy only works when it's allowed in the room. And post 2022, the room is the whole world. It's everywhere'.

I am certain that remote work, whether fully remote or hybrid remote, will be the way we work, in all sectors, in all professions where the work itself can be done independent of location. It gives us too many benefits to be cast aside, and health- and climate-related disruptions are likely to become more frequent and require it again the way we needed it during the Covid-19 pandemic. In the future, remote work will be one of our most important business continuity levers. And if we have leaders who can empathize and connect, we will have remote workers who bring their best selves to their jobs.

If we have leaders who understand the difference between *connection urgency* and *communication patience*, we have leaders who spend time on the things that matter when we work from a distance, the things that engender meaning, joy, faith, clarity, and belonging. When work feels like this, we want to do more than we're asked to do. Discretionary effort comes easily. Our creativity and passion flows. Imagine a business with a distributed workforce all feeling this way.

At the end of my career, I will only ever remember the people. Maybe you feel the same way. Leadership is a creative act, an act of creating a work experience that helps an employee grow, learn, achieve, and succeed. What a privilege it has been for me to lead people for the past almost 30 years, to play whatever small role I could in helping each one of them live the professional lives they imagined for themselves. With remote work, leadership must be seen through a new human-centered prism. While remote work makes serendipity more difficult, it makes intention more important, and the result is far richer. As I said earlier in the book, it's a fallacy to think that being physically located in the same building will make us more connected to each other. You can pass a person in an office for years and not know who they are. We have all done that. Remote work is our invitation to know the people we do our jobs with, to *really* know them, both while remote and on the occasions when we meet in person.

I wish you, as remote and hybrid leaders, all the success in the world. You can now empathize with your remote and hybrid employees through the case studies and behavioral research we reviewed in Part One. Your remote leadership behavior blueprints in Part Two are your tools to take compassionate action, using the data of emotions as your guide.

I believe that now is one of the most exciting times to lead in human history. We have vast challenges ahead, but we have the ingenuity to rise to every challenge. We just need to be brave. We just need to be human.

Good luck!

RESOURCE I: REMOTE WORK EMPATHY SCANS

Boredom (Chapter 2)

When your employee is bored or has reached enough of a deep sense of boredom that you would consider it 'boreout', he or she will likely display these behaviors:

+ asks for different work to do;
+ asks why what they are doing is important;
+ allows scope creep (i.e., saying 'yes' to everything) to bring new content into their job;
+ takes longer to deliver work, which you may at first see as laziness.

Depression (Chapter 3)

Aside from open conversation, there are some signs worth looking out for that your employee is coping with something challenging:

+ contributes less in meetings than in the past;
+ expresses worry or doubt on a regular basis;
+ seems reluctant to collaborate;
+ delivers work that is not up to their usual standard and misses deadlines.

Guilt (Chapter 4)

Born out of fear, guilt, and suspicion, your employee will exhibit these compensatory behaviors to try to convince you that they are worth their weight, especially when they work from home:

+ responds to emails outside of business hours and on vacation;
+ creates unnecessary urgency and sets unrealistic deadlines for projects they manage;
+ feels the need to explain how they are using their time, both work and personal;
+ requests fractions of paid leave to do things like seeing a doctor or doesn't use all their holiday allocation.

Paranoia (Chapter 5)

Paranoia is a normal reaction to stress, sometimes from a lack of clarity and equity as a remote worker. Be on the lookout for some of these behaviors:

+ expresses frequent doubts about self-worth and feelings of exclusion;
+ adopts tactics to conserve resources – possibly concealing information from you and others;
+ frequently asks about the whereabouts and meetings of other members of the team;
+ proposes or actively pursues interactions with more senior executives to increase proximity.

Loneliness (Chapter 6)

As a manager, how do you know if your employee is suffering from remote work-induced loneliness? Here are a few of the signals:

+ has limited personal connections or friends in the company;
+ demonstrates counterproductive behavior, such as under preparing for meetings;
+ shows signs of stress through uncharacteristic actions or expressions;
+ has had a change at home that contributes to more loneliness, such as the departure of a roommate, child, or spouse, or the loss of a family member or pet.

RESOURCE II: DISCUSSION STARTERS

Leadership behavior blueprint #1: Checking in

1. How are you?
2. What has happened this week that you're excited about?
3. What did you learn from a customer this week?
4. What is one thing that has made you feel closer to your career aspirations this week?
5. What change are you part of right now and how do you feel about it?

Leadership behavior blueprint #2: Communicating with optimism

1. Tell me about a change you're going through and the opportunities it will give you.
2. What didn't work out this week and what did you discover?
3. What is one thing in our business that could use a change for the better?
4. Is there something that happened this week that the team should celebrate?
5. What is the most fun you've had this week – at work or outside of work?

Leadership behavior blueprint #3: Building trust

1. What makes you feel most trusted at work and do you feel that you are?
2. Is there any accomplishment from this week you want to make sure I know?
3. Is there anything you think I should be highlighting to our executives?
4. How confident do you feel about X project? How can I help?
5. How can I be delegating more effectively to you?

Leadership behavior blueprint #4: Setting boundaries

1. Is your current schedule clearly aligned to your goals?
2. Is there any project you're working on that needs to be communicated more across the company?
3. Can work keep going with other members of the team while you're offline? How can we improve that?
4. What is one thing you can stop doing?
5. Who is accountable to you and are they delivering?

Leadership behavior blueprint #5: Managing performance

1. What goal is at risk, and do you know why?
2. What goal has already been accomplished, and what new one can we replace it with?
3. How will you measure X? [where 'X' is any task or project]
4. Who helped you achieve that milestone and how?
5. What type of mentor at our company would be most helpful to you?

RESOURCE III: LEADERSHIP BEHAVIOR BLUEPRINTS

Emotion: Boredom (Chapter 2); **Counterpoint emotion:** Meaning

Leadership behavior blueprint #1: Checking in (Chapter 7)

+ *Dimension #1*: Start with 'How are you?' and leave time for the answer.
+ *Dimension #2*: Discuss purpose.
+ *Dimension #3*: Encourage and facilitate development.
+ *Dimension #4*: Help your team effect positive change.
+ *Dimension #5*: Don't forget that everything you do means something to a customer.

Emotion: Depression (Chapter 3); **Counterpoint emotion:** Joy

Leadership behavior blueprint #2: Communicating with optimism (Chapter 8)

+ *Dimension #1*: Be excited (even joyful) about change and what it means for your team.
+ *Dimension #2*: Celebrate the wonder of both wins and losses.
+ *Dimension #3*: Make time for play.

+ *Dimension #4*: Share each other's joy.
+ *Dimension #5*: Laugh at yourself first and foremost.

Emotion: Guilt (Chapter 4); **Counterpoint emotion:** Faith

Leadership behavior blueprint #3: Building trust (Chapter 9)

+ *Dimension #1*: Champion autonomous scheduling, not mandated flexibility.
+ *Dimension #2*: Prioritize care over inconvenience.
+ *Dimension #3*: Develop a culture of psychological safety (and develop a culture).
+ *Dimension #4*: Delegate and keep your distance.
+ *Dimension #5*: Attribute credit to your employees at senior levels.

Emotion: Paranoia (Chapter 5); **Counterpoint emotion:** Clarity

Leadership behavior blueprint #4: Setting boundaries (Chapter 10)

+ *Dimension #1*: Enable your teams to work asynchronously.
+ *Dimension #2*: Practice communication patience.
+ *Dimension #3*: Overcommunicate. And then communicate again.
+ *Dimension #4*: Hold people accountable.
+ *Dimension #5*: Teach your team to say 'no' or at least 'not right now'.

Emotion: Loneliness (Chapter 6); **Counterpoint emotion:** Belonging

Leadership behavior blueprint #5: Managing performance (Chapter 11)

+ *Dimension #1*: Highlight achievements and hearsay.
+ *Dimension #2*: Measure everything – what gets measured gets done.
+ *Dimension #3*: Talk about slippage before it becomes an ongoing trend.
+ *Dimension #4*: Connect work output to team, department, and company vision and purpose.
+ *Dimension #5*: Encourage mentorship from elsewhere in the company.

APPENDIX A:
LOW CARBON STRATEGIES
FOR REMOTE WORK

A recent study from MIT revealed that 96% of the carbon footprint of a virtual meeting is streaming video of yourself to others, and them to you. The carbon footprint comes from the energy needed to keep broadband servers cool. Even running a Google search pings a server with each search and requires some cooling. Worldwide we search Google 3.5 billion times *every single day*, and Google accounts for over 40% of the internet's carbon footprint. When you consider the millions of people working remotely and the millions of hours we are likely streaming video of ourselves during conference calls or searching for something on Google, the carbon impact quickly becomes significant.

The assumption is that remote work is a big win for the planet, mainly because we aren't commuting back and forth from home to office. But is it? It turns out that it depends on where you live, the availability of public transportation, how large your home is, how much you use your A/C or heating, how renewable your home's electricity supply is, how often you stream yourself in video calls, and still many other factors.

So it isn't always a win for the planet. Very often, the planetary cost of us all being at home, climatizing a home space only for ourselves, is meaningful enough to, in some cases, negate the climate benefits of not commuting.

It's important that companies understand the carbon impact of remote work and begin crafting strategies to bring it down. Here are some places to start:

1. **Measure the carbon impact of your remote workforce and include it as part of your company's Scope 3 emissions.** Scope 3 emissions are the part of a company's carbon footprint that are not directly within the company's control but that a company still bears some responsibility for creating. Know how many employee days (No. of employees × No. of remote dates) of remote work are happening across your workforce and in what cities. Understand power sources in those areas – clean energy or fossil fuel-based? Estimate household energy in those locations, including internet, electricity, heating, and cooling.

2. **Develop education and incentives or use gamification to help remote employees use less resources at home.** Are there schemes offered by local power companies to shift the source of power from fossil fuels to renewables? Is offsetting the cost of this switch something your company can include in employees' benefit packages? Using gamification is an excellent way to help the company's carbon footprint but also drive employee engagement. Identify work-away locations with exceptionally clean power grids and create a program where your employees can work away for six, eight, or ten weeks in a location where the power they need to work is all coming from a renewable source. Rather than bringing clean power to the market, having a remote workforce means you can bring the market to the clean power. Imagine that!

3. **Encourage asynchronous work where it fits a project or team.** When all of us are online all at the same time, the cooling load on data servers peaks. If your team can work asynchronously – online at hours that are convenient for them but may not be the 'core business' hours of 9 to 5 – you're actually helping to remove the cooling load on servers. So your employee gets the flexibility they need, and servers are cooler.

4. **Be intentional about travel and the frequency of in-person time.** Absolutely teams need time to be together, but imagine the difference it would make if you planned three or four trips a year for your team instead of monthly in-person meetings. Quarterly gatherings give everyone a chance to see each other with enough frequency that relationships strengthen, and time lost on frequent travel is gained back in work productivity. These quarterly in-person gatherings can be given the appropriate amount of thought and planning as well. How often have you traveled for a meeting, having just seen many of the same people in the last meeting only a few weeks ago, and the pace of work is so hectic that nobody had time to do the pre-reading or even think about why they are in the room together? Sounds familiar, doesn't it? Be intentional about in-person time, and don't feel you have to cram your schedule with it. You don't.

APPENDIX B: DIVERSITY AND INCLUSION CONSIDERATIONS FOR REMOTE WORK

All of us who could work remotely went to our home offices in March 2020 and, as of the time of writing, many of us are still there. Most people understandably struggled with the transition because it collided with a transition of kids being sent home from school to study remotely at the same time. The younger the kids were, the more difficult it was for teachers to keep them engaged through a Zoom screen, and the burden fell on parents to keep their children's education on track.

I was lucky in that my children were older and could handle Zoom learning, even if they didn't like it. I was also lucky because I had been working from home full time already for three years, so, for me personally, my own work set-up didn't change. But one important thing did get much better: everyone else started working remotely, too. Gone were meetings where a large group was gathered in a conference room and I was one of only a few people joining remotely, struggling to see or hear what was going on in the room. Gone were the start of meetings that were nothing more than an indecipherable buzz of conversation of people talking about kids and vacations and what they just ate for lunch (together) while I waited at my desk for the actual meeting to start. Suddenly every meeting was conducted on an even playing field, with each person occupying a square in my screen and each side comment audible or legible in a chat thread in the meeting. Frankly, I loved it. Work got much better.

I spoke to one seasoned human resources professional I'll call Maria, a black female, who has worked at both a large international retailer and a start-up and experienced remote work at both. In both cases, she wasn't able to relocate for the jobs but was hired because the role was difficult to fill. At the retailer, pre-pandemic, she was told outright that her absence wouldn't be well tolerated by the rest of her colleagues who came into the office in person. So she traveled frequently, one week out of the month. She was often away from her family and young children to make it work, which she did for almost three years.

At the start-up, Maria is part of a small population, only 2% of the workforce, who is 'designated remote'. As a start-up, the company feels that in-person work is vital to collaboration and is working on nurturing a fully in-person culture. She acknowledged the inconvenience to the company founders that this 'designated remote' group exists at all. But where does that leave her? She acknowledged the conundrum: how could she champion an in-person culture if she were 'designated remote' herself? Was she facing likely redundancy or managed attrition? By not making a decision, the company was leaving that 2%, which included her, to wither on its human resource vine.

The lesson in this story for your diversity and inclusion plans is that, if you have even *one person* who is remote, you need to take remote policies and practices into account. You need to ensure you are leveling the playing field. And we know that non-white workers are more interested in working from home, so taking care of your remote population has to be integral to your diversity and inclusion strategy because that's more often where your diverse workforce will be.

Roberta Sawatzky, Professor of HR and Management at the Okanagan School of Business, Okanagan College in British Columbia, says that hybrid definitions of work are now so varied that leaders are wise to default to having a 'digital first' mindset in all situations. This means that team building, communication, and meetings need to be structured with a digital platform as the default 'place'.

Yin Rani, CEO of the milk industry organization MilkPEP in the US, says that, when everyone was fully remote, inclusion was much easier. Now her organization is experimenting with different designated days in the office, but everyone needs something different. Who do you make happy? She has observed in the wider talent marketplace that people's lives moved on during the pandemic, and designated in-office days seem to have left some people feeling that resigning is their only option.

There are even some companies who are not only abandoning any pretense of inclusion but also forcing some of their best people to quit with draconian ultimatums. I spoke to a woman I'll call Brenda who worked as a training and merchandising strategist for a specialty retailer in the US. The retailer's mission meant the world to Brenda, and she was an example of a lucky person whose life mission and work mission were fully aligned. As with most companies, Brenda and other employees did the majority of their work from home during the pandemic. After the pandemic, her company decided that everyone had to move to the company's headquarters city and work full time in person, which was thousands of miles from Brenda's home. If an employee couldn't make the move, they had to commit to weekly travel and working more than 40 hours per week. Brenda knew it would compromise her quality of life and well-being so much that she felt her only option was to resign. What a valuable, mission-driven employee the company lost by choosing exclusion.

I think it's important not to lose what we gained during the pandemic-era remote working when it comes to making all remote employees feel included. In a company's diversity and inclusion strategy, inclusion of the remote and hybrid employee needs to be part of the playbook. These are the five areas I'd suggest organizational design teams focus on to ensure their remote and hybrid workforce has an equal seat at the table:

1. **Know your local regulations.** At the time of writing, the Netherlands has passed a law giving people the right to work remotely, meaning a company cannot turn down a reasonable request for accommodation to work remotely. We will likely see more countries passing similar regulations, especially those that already have favorable employee rights laws, such as Ireland's 'Right to Disconnect' and France's similar law about employees not being obligated to send or reply to emails after business hours.

2. **Monitor the diversity profile of your remote employees.** Based on the latest research on the demographic profile of who tends to prefer remote work, your remote population will likely skew more to women and minorities. Make sure they have equal access to the resources specifically designed to support them. For example, if you have a panel on neurodiversity taking place in your office, can your neurodiverse remote employees watch the panel from home? You'd be surprised how often the most well-meaning event organizer will forget the people at home.

3. **Encourage diversity amongst your remote work population.** Encourage men and senior executives to take advantage of remote work as a way to diversify the population of people working from home. This helps create empathy for remote employees across all levels of the organization and prevents a remote work stigma from befalling any specific minority population.

4. **Avoid hybrid meetings where some participants are at home and some are in the office.** As I described above from my pre-pandemic remote work experience, in hybrid meetings the person joining from home will struggle to follow what's happening in a conference room. There will be side conversations, trouble with mics, and some people talking who are off camera.

If you really can't avoid hybrid meetings, and it's likely given the growing popularity of hybrid working, then it helps if everyone in the in-person meeting is joining on their laptop with camera on and volume off, with a master mic in the conference room dialed into the virtual meeting too. The person working at home can now see every person in the conference room on each person's individual laptop screen and watch them talking, as well as type messages into the meeting chat if necessary, just as if they were sitting side by side.

At Thomas International, CEO Sabby Gill described to me how meetings are handled as a matter of inclusion: if everyone is in the office and there's even one person joining the meeting remotely, everyone finds a place in the building where they can join the meeting online and that is how the meeting is conducted. In the same vein, they will sometimes purposely plan all-hands meetings for a day when they know that nobody will be in the office, so the meeting will be 100% virtual by default.

5. **Audit the career and salary progression of your remote work population on a regular basis.** Are fully remote employees progressing in terms of compensation and promotion at the same rate as fully in-office or hybrid employees? Compare across the three populations,

identify discrepancies, and have a plan to correct. Take the same cut of employee engagement scores and retention rates and understand and correct imbalances.

ACKNOWLEDGMENTS

The idea for this book began over afternoon tea in Dublin with my friend Frederique Murphy. Frederique is an author, a speaker, and an expert in neuroscience. She has dedicated her life to teaching people how to push through fears and doubts to pursue their passions – how to adopt what she calls a 'mountain moving mindset'. In Dublin that day, she told me my leadership voice needed to be heard. I had a hundred reasons why it didn't, but she gently refused to take 'no' for an answer. Thanks to her, this book is in your hands. Frederique, I hope I have fulfilled your expectations and put a voice into the world that will help many leaders. I can now say 'I'm doing it!' because you taught me how. From the bottom of my heart, thank you for helping me lead beyond my edge.

I owe so many thanks to Alison Jones at Practical Inspiration Publishing and her caring and patient team, particularly Shell Cooper, Judith Wise, Nim Moorthy, Frances Staton, and Michelle Charman. I asked all the dumb questions and they answered them with exceptional cheer. I am so grateful they felt compelled to invest commercial resources in my words and ideas. Nothing fills a writer with more feeling of possibility than that.

Thank you to Lisette Sutherland for lending her voice to this book's mission by writing such a beautiful and insightful foreword. With her fabulous body of work at Collaboration Superpowers and her wonderful book *Work Together Anywhere*, she has blazed a path in this new world of work that the rest of us can follow confidently. I am so grateful for her participation in this book, and I'm thankful that she shared her wisdom in these pages and in her own.

Thanks from the bottom of my heart to my beta readers for their thoughtful comments, suggestions, and support: Jack Gilden, Sabby Gill, Susan Harris, Gabe Karp, Beatriz Martín-Luquero, Chaya Mistry, Elisa Moscolin, Amy Tomlinson, and Salila Yohn. They were the first to see what I was excavating from deep in my heart and mind, and their expertise, ideas, and feedback have made the book so much better. They helped me see myself and my message with so much more clarity. Thank you also to my development editor Kate Llewellyn for her enthusiasm and early guidance, which helped land the big ideas in a more coherent way. Thank you to Nicky Brown for her consummate skill in copyediting and even more in her patience with a fiddly writer.

Thank you to the many inspiring people who agreed to sit for an interview with me and have their advice, experience, and reflections included in these pages: Arne Beitlich, Amy Blankson, Andrew Bolton, Ilona Brannen, Leslie Carruthers, Thomas Cheney, Agnieszka Cislo, Colleen Crino, Ricardo Fernandez, Chris Flack, Allison Gabriel, Sabby Gill, Sarah Hawley, Rowena Hennigan, Shawn Kanungo, Gabe Karp, Laraine Miller, Chaya Mistry, Darren Murph, Virang Patel, Araceli Pison, Cristiana Pruteanu, Cathal Quinlan, Yin Rani, John Riordan, Jennifer Sakaguchi, Roberta Sawatzky, Laura Schwarz, Susan Sobbott, Valentina Thörner, Amy Tomlinson, Scott Wharton, and five people whose stories I have used pseudonymously or anonymously. Their courage and candor will make us all stronger leaders. Our conversations and their support of this book's mission have filled me with so much reward and satisfaction.

A huge amount of thanks go especially to two women I've never met, but whose selfless investment in this project has filled me with so much gratitude and been one of my most powerful lessons about building meaningful connections despite distance, and despite even familiarity: Rowena Hennigan, an expert in remote work and wellness, who responded to a cold direct message on LinkedIn, opening up her wealth of contacts and making introductions for me with some of the most fascinating people I've ever talked to; and Aneta Ardelian Kuzma, who recorded a mantra for me and for the book, a mantra I listened to before every writing session. I hope the book they both helped me put out into the world is something they can be proud of having supported.

Thank you to all my colleagues and collaborators over the past three decades, you know who you are. When it's all done, I will only ever remember you. You've taught me everything. You've filled every day with fun and meaning.

To my mom, Liz Tomlinson – thank you for telling me all those great stories about dad and for being the inspiring human you are. I clearly didn't learn about being human on my own.

To my sons, Julian and Ian – thank you for being interested in what I was doing and being impressed by the word count. Making you proud of your mom is what keeps me going.

Thank you to all my Tomlinson and Romo family for always cheering me on.

And to my husband, Agustin – thank you for believing in me. Thank you for finding the humor in everything, especially deadlines. Thank you for being good at drawing circles. I fell in love with you because of how much you care about other people. What you have taught me about being human has inspired every word and makes me so proud to be your wife. Con amor, siempre.

BIBLIOGRAPHY

Preface

American Psychiatric Association. 'As Americans begin to return to the office, views on workplace mental health are mixed.' May 20, 2021. www.psychiatry.org/newsroom/news-releases/as-americans-begin-to-return-to-the-office-views-on-workplace-mental-health-are-mixed

Bloom, N., Liang, J., Roberts, J., and Ying, Z. 'Does working from home work? Evidence from a Chinese experiment.' *The Quarterly Journal of Economics* 130, no. 1 (2015): 165–218. https://doi.org/10.1093/qje/qju032

Crino, C. Interview with the author. Virtual. June 24, 2022.

Introduction

Parelli. 'Parelli Natural Horsemanship.' https://shopus.parelli.com/

Parker, K., and Horowitz, J. 'Majority of workers who quit a job in 2021 cite low pay, no opportunities for advancement, feeling disrespected.' March 9, 2022. Pew Research Center. www.pewresearch.org/fact-tank/2022/03/09/majority-of-workers-who-quit-a-job-in-2021-cite-low-pay-no-opportunities-for-advancement-feeling-disrespected

Sobbott, S. Interview with the author. Virtual. September 1, 2022.

Wiles, J. 'Great resignation or not, money won't fix all your talent problems.' December 9, 2021. Gartner. www.gartner.com/en/articles/great-resignation-or-not-money-won-t-fix-all-your-talent-problems

1. Between one work world and the next

Anthony, C. (host). 'Kenneth Chenault.' *What's in your glass?* (podcast). February 10, 2022. https://podcasts.apple.com/us/podcast/kenneth-chenault/id1576873726?I=1000550651269

Barsade, S., and O'Neill, O. 'What's love got to do with it? A longitudinal study of the culture of companionate love and employee and client outcomes in a long-term care setting.' *Administrative Science Quarterly* 59 (2014): 551–598. https://doi.org/10.1177/0001839214538636

Belmonte, A. 'Organizational psychologist explains why "hybrid is the future" of the workplace.' July 22, 2022. Yahoo! Finance. https://finance.yahoo.com/news/organizational-psychologist-explains-why-hybrid-is-the-future-of-the-workplace-165549543.html

Bergland, C. 'To boost creativity, cultivate empathy.' February 3, 2021. *Psychology Today.* www.psychologytoday.com/us/blog/the-athletes-way/202102/boost-creativity-cultivate-empathy

Brown, B. *Dare to lead.* New York: Random House, 2018.

Businessolver. '2021 State of workplace empathy.' https://resources.businessolver.com/c/2021-empathy-exec-summ?x=OE03jO

Business Wire. 'Ryan Reynolds announces new nonprofit, The Creative Ladder, to make creative marketing careers more accessible to underrepresented communities.' June 21, 2022.

www.businesswire.com/news/home/20220621005394/en/ Ryan-Reynolds-Announces-New-Nonprofit-The-Creative-Ladder-to-Make-Creative-Marketing-Careers-More-Accessible-to-Underrepresented-Communities

Dam, R., and Siang, T. 'What is empathy and why is it so important to design thinking?' Interaction Design Foundation. www.interaction-design.org/literature/article/design-thinking-getting-started-with-empathy

Design Management Institute. '2015 dmi: Design value index results and commentary.' www.dmi.org/page/2015DVIandOTW

De Waal, F. 'The evolution of empathy.' September 1, 2005. *Greater Good Magazine.* University of California, Berkeley. https://greatergood.berkeley.edu/article/item/the_evolution_of_empathy

Ernst & Young. 'New EY Consulting survey confirms 90% of US workers believe empathetic leadership leads to higher job satisfaction and 79% agree it decreases employee turnover.' October 14, 2021. www.ey.com/en_us/news/2021/09/ey-empathy-in-business-survey

Goleman, D. 'Hot to help: When can empathy move us to action.' March 1, 2008. *Greater Good Magazine.* University of California, Berkeley. https://greatergood.berkeley.edu/article/item/hot_to_help

Greater Good Magazine. 'What is empathy?' University of California, Berkeley. https://greatergood.berkeley.edu/topic/empathy/definition

Hawley, S. Interview with the author. Virtual. August 23, 2022.

JD Supra. 'The changing workplace: Work from home accommodations.' August 12, 2022. www.jdsupra.com/legalnews/the-changing-workplace-work-from-home-7637178/

Marston, W. *The emotions of normal people.* London: Kegan Paul, Trench, Turner & Co. Ltd, 1928.

Martín-Luquero, B. Interview with the author. Virtual. June 6, 2022.

McKinsey & Company. 'The emotion archive.' August 27, 2020. www.mckinsey.com/business-functions/mckinsey-design/how-we-help-clients/design-blog/the-emotion-archive-finding-global-empathy-in-a-challenging-time

Milinkovic, M. 'The leadership gap: 20 revealing male vs female CEO statistics.' March 11, 2022. SmallBizGenius. www.smallbizgenius.net/by-the-numbers/male-vs-female-ceo-statistics/#gref

Murph, D. LinkedIn profile. www.linkedin.com/in/darrenmurph/

Netflix. 'Brené Brown: The call to courage.' 2018. Video, 1:30. www.netflix.com/title/81010166

Netflix. 'The Crown: Season 1, Episode 1.' November 4, 2016. Video. www.netflix.com/title/80025678

Riordan, J. Interview with the author. Virtual. July 21, 2022.

Risen, C. 'Sigal Barsade, 56, dies; Argued that it's OK to show emotions at work.' February 13, 2022. *The New York Times.* www.nytimes.com/2022/02/13/business/sigal-barsade-dead.html

Roy, A. 'Arundhati Roy: The pandemic is a portal.' April 3, 2020. *The Financial Times.* www.ft.com/content/10d8f5e8-74eb-11ea-95fe-fcd274e920ca

Schwarz, L. Interview with the author. Virtual. August 24, 2022.

Simon-Thomas, E. 'Which factors shape our empathy.' July 31, 2017. *Greater Good Magazine.* University of California, Berkeley. https://greatergood.berkeley.edu/article/item/which_factors_shape_our_empathy

Van Bommel, T. 'The power of empathy in times of crisis and beyond.' Catalyst. www.catalyst.org/reports/empathy-work-strategy-crisis

Weisenthal, J. 'We love what Warren Buffett says about life, luck and winning the "ovarian lottery".' December 10, 2013. Business Insider. www.businessinsider.com/warren-buffett-on-the-ovarian-lottery-2013-12

2. Boredom: How home office monotony leads to 'boreout'

Bloom, N., Liang, J., Roberts, J., and Ying, Z. 'Does working from home work? Evidence from a Chinese experiment.' *The Quarterly Journal of Economics* 130, no. 1 (2015): 165–218. https://doi.org/10.1093/qje/qju032

Bolton, A. Interview with the author. Virtual. June 23, 2022.

Bradley, S. 'Why more young people are turning to nihilism.' April 25, 2022. *Huck.* www.huckmag.com/perspectives/why-more-young-people-are-turning-to-nihilism/

Cable, D. *Alive at work.* Boston: Harvard Business Review Press, 2019.

Crino, C. Interview with the author. June 24, 2022.

iResearchNet. 'Boredom at work.' http://psychology.iresearchnet. com/industrial-organizational-psychology/job-satisfaction/ boredom-at-work/

Milosevic, Y. 'This is what boreout looks like.' July 1, 2021. Blacklight blog. https://theblacklight.co/2021/07/01/boreout-syndrome/

Navarrete, S. 'Workplace skills, hiring, and productivity in a post-pandemic UK.' August 3, 2021. Capterra blog. www.capterra. co.uk/blog/1948/workplace-skills-hiring-productivity-post-pandemic-uk

Pendell, R. 'The world's $7.8 trillion workplace problem.' June 14, 2022. Gallup Workplace. www.gallup.com/workplace/393497/ world-trillion-workplace-problem.aspx

Pruteanu, C. Interview with the author. Virtual. June 2, 2022.

Reddit. r/nihilism. www.reddit.com/r/nihilism/

Schnitzer, K. 'What is boreout and why you may be suffering from it right now?' August 31, 2020. The Ladders blog. www. theladders.com/career-advice/what-is-boreout-and-why-you-may-be-suffering-from-it-right-now

Udemy. 'Udemy in depth: 2016 Workplace boredom report.' https://research.udemy.com/research_report/2016-workplace-boredom-report/

3. Depression: How personal crises make working alone a special challenge

Buckner, D. 'The working-at-home blues: Loneliness, depression a risk for those who are isolated.' April 24, 2019. CBC News. www.cbc.ca/news/business/working-at-home-isolation-1.5103498

Oakman, J., Kinsman, N., Stuckey, R., Graham, M., and Weale, V. 'A rapid review of mental and physical health effects of working at home: How do we optimize health?' *BMC Public Health* 20, 1825 (2020). https://doi.org/10.1186/s12889-020-09875-z

Office for National Statistics (UK). 'Coronavirus and depression in adults, Great Britain: July to August 2021.' www.ons.gov.uk/peoplepopulationandcommunity/wellbeing/articles/coronavirusanddepressioninadultsgreatbritain/julytoaugust2021

4. Guilt: How we punish ourselves amid the blurred boundaries of home and office

Bloom, N., Liang, J., Roberts, J., and Ying, Z. 'Does working from home work? Evidence from a Chinese experiment.' *The Quarterly Journal of Economics* 130, no. 1 (2015): 165–218. https://doi.org/10.1093/qje/qju032

Filabi, A., and Hurley, R. 'The paradox of employee surveillance.' February 18, 2019. *Behavioral Scientist.* https://behavioralscientist.org/the-paradox-of-employee-surveillance/

Gabriel, A. Interview with the author. July 14, 2022.

GitLab. 'Hybrid-remote: Understanding nuances and pitfalls.' https://about.gitlab.com/company/culture/all-remote/hybrid-remote/

Glassdoor. 'American Express work from home.' www.glassdoor.com/Benefits/American-Express-Work-From-Home-US-BNFT152_E35_N1_IP5.htm

Hemp, P. 'Presenteeism: At work – but out of it.' October 2004. *Harvard Business Review.* https://hbr.org/2004/10/presenteeism-at-work-but-out-of-it

Jacobs, E. 'The end of sick days: Has WFH made it harder to take time off?' April 18, 2022. *Financial Times.* www.ft.com/content/bc9e39ce-8762-4e70-8aa2-2e33b23b80fe

Johnson, K. 'How to overcome the work-from-home guilt.' May 9, 2021. Claromentis blog. www.claromentis.com/blog/how-to-overcome-work-from-home-guilt/

Migliano, S., and O'Donnell, C. 'Employee surveillance software demand up 58% since pandemic started.' August 8, 2022. Top VPN blog. www.top10vpn.com/research/covid-employee-surveillance/

Moore, Danielle. 'People working from home still feel guilty about taking a lunch break.' September 21, 2020. New York Post. https://nypost.com/2020/09/21/people-working-from-home-feel-guilty-about-taking-breaks-and-some-dont-even-take-a-lunch-break/

Mullenweg, M. 'Coronavirus and the remote work experiment no one asked for.' March 5, 2020. Matt Mullenweg blog. https://ma.tt/2020/03/coronavirus-remote-work/

Murph, D. Interview with the author. Virtual. July 14, 2022.

Parker, S., Knight, C., and Keller, A. 'Remote managers are having trust issues.' July 30, 2020. *Harvard Business Review.*

https://hbr.org/2020/07/remote-managers-are-having-trust-issues

Pearson, E. 'How to ease work-from-home guilt.' January 7, 2021. *Entrepreneur.* www.entrepreneur.com/article/361461

Qualitative Mind. 'Is social loafing worse in online meetings?' May 14, 2020. www.qualitativemind.com/is-social-loafing-worse-in-online-meetings/

Reddit. 'Anyone else experience guilt with work from home and not being busy 100% of the time?' r/jobs. www.reddit.com/r/jobs/comments/iumsx8/anyone_else_experience_guilt_with_work_from_home/

Rushe, D. 'Elon Musk tells employees to return to the office or "pretend to work somewhere else".' June 1, 2022. *The Guardian.* www.theguardian.com/technology/2022/jun/01/elon-musk-return-to-office-pretend-to-work-somewhere-else

Sobbott, S. Interview with the author. Virtual. September 1, 2022.

Stanford Institute for Economic Policy Research. 'How working from home works out.' https://siepr.stanford.edu/publications/policy-brief/how-working-home-works-out

US Department of Labor. 'Sick Leave.' www.dol.gov/general/topic/workhours/sickleave

5. Paranoia: How we fear being 'out of sight, out of mind'

Aware. 'What if you could automatically measure the voice of the employee, getting an authentic reflection of how your workforce feels?' www.awarehq.com/people-insights

Bloom, N., Liang, J., Roberts, J., and Ying, Z. 'Does working from home work? Evidence from a Chinese experiment.' *The Quarterly Journal of Economics* 130, no. 1 (2015): 165–218. https://doi.org/10.1093/qje/qju032

ExpressVPN. 'ExpressVPN survey reveals the extent of surveillance on the remote workforce.' December 1, 2021. www.expressvpn.com/blog/expressvpn-survey-surveillance-on-the-remote-workforce/#ethics

Grose, J. 'Is remote work making us paranoid?' April 30, 2021. *The New York Times.* www.nytimes.com/2021/01/13/style/is-remote-work-making-us-paranoid.html

Heller, J. *Catch-22: A novel.* New York: The Modern Library, 1961.

Hirsch, A. 'Preventing proximity bias in a hybrid workplace.' March 22, 2022. Society for Human Resource Management blog. www.shrm.org/resourcesandtools/hr-topics/employee-relations/pages/preventing-proximity-bias-in-a-hybrid-workplace.aspx

Kingston, J.L., Schlier, B., Ellett, L., So, S.H., Gaudiano, B.A., Morris, E.M.J., and Lincoln, T.M. 'The Pandemic Paranoia Scale (PPS): Factor structure and measurement invariance across languages.' *Psychological Medicine* (December 9, 2021): 1–10. https://doi.org/10.1017/S0033291721004633

Krkovic, K., Nowak, U., Kammerer, M., Bott, A., and Lincoln, T. 'Aberrant adapting of beliefs under stress: A mechanism relevant to the formation of paranoia?' September 14, 2021. *Psychological Medicine,* 1–10. https://doi.org/10.1017/S0033291721003524

Mækelæ, M., Reggev, N., Defelipe, R., Dutra, N., Tamayo, R.M., Klevjer, K., and Pfuhl, G. 'Identifying resilience factors of distress and paranoia during the COVID-19 outbreak in five countries.' June 10, 2021. *Frontiers in Psychology* 12. https://doi.org/10.3389/fpsyg.2021.661149

Mearian, L. 'Women, minorities less inclined to return to office, face "proximity bias".' March 9, 2022. *Computer World.* www.computerworld.com/article/3652592/women-people-of-color-less-likely-to-want-to-return-to-office.html

Mind. 'What is paranoia?' www.mind.org.uk/information-support/types-of-mental-health-problems/paranoia/about-paranoia/

PR Newswire. 'Virtual reality: Remote employees experience more workplace politics than onsite teammates.' www.prnewswire.com/news-releases/virtual-reality-remote-employees-experience-more-workplace-politics-than-onsite-teammates-300548594.html

6. Loneliness: How remote work challenges our human need for connection

American Psychiatric Association. 'As Americans begin to return to the office, views on workplace mental health are mixed.' May 20, 2021. www.psychiatry.org/newsroom/news-releases/as-americans-begin-to-return-to-the-office-views-on-workplace-mental-health-are-mixed

Becker, W.J., Belkin, L.Y., Tuskey, S.E., and Conroy, S.A. 'Surviving remotely: How job control and loneliness during a forced shift to remote work impacted employee work behaviors and well-being.' *Human Resource Management* 61, no. 4 (2022): 449–464. https://doi.org/10.1002/hrm.22102

Buffer. '2022 State of remote work.' https://buffer.com/state-of-remote-work/2022

Flack, C. Interview with the author. Virtual. July 7, 2022.

Hennigan, R. 'Loneliness, disconnection and vulnerable leadership.' May 12, 2022. Remote Work Digest. www.linkedin.com/pulse/loneliness-vulnerable-leadership-rowena-hennigan-she-her-/

Murthy, V. 'Work and the loneliness epidemic.' September 26, 2017. *Harvard Business Review*. https://hbr.org/2017/09/work-and-the-loneliness-epidemic

Rath, T., and Harter, J. 'Your friends and your social well-being.' August 19, 2010. *Gallup Business Journal*. https://news.gallup.com/businessjournal/127043/friends-social-wellbeing.aspx

Riordan, J. Interview with the author. Virtual. July 21, 2022.

Tomlinson, A. Interview with the author. Virtual. September 15, 2022.

Total Jobs. 'Lockdown loneliness and the collapse of social life at work.' www.totaljobs.com/advice/lockdown-loneliness-the-collapse-of-social-life-at-work

7. Leadership behavior blueprint #1: Checking in

Brannen, I. Interview with the author. Virtual. August 26, 2022.

Carruthers, L. Interview with the author. Virtual. June 2, 2022.

Fernandez, R. Interview with the author. Virtual. June 20, 2022.

Hennigan, R. Interview with the author. Virtual. August 23, 2022.

Peters, T.J., and Waterman, R.H. *In search of excellence: Lessons from America's best-run companies.* New York: Harper & Row, 1982.

Sobbott, S. Interview with the author. Virtual. September 1, 2022.

Thörner, V. Interview with the author. Virtual. August 26, 2022.

Wharton, S. Interview with the author. Virtual. June 23, 2022.

8. Leadership behavior blueprint #2: Communicating with optimism

Abbasi, J. 'Why friends make us happier, healthier people.' The Upside by Twill. www.happify.com/hd/why-friends-make-us-happier/

Barsade, S. 'The ripple effect: Emotional contagion in groups.' *Yale School of Management Working Papers* 47 (2001). https://doi.org/10.2139/ssrn.250894

Cable, D. *Alive at work.* Boston: Harvard Business Review Press, 2019.

Crino, C. Interview with the author. Virtual. June 24, 2022.

Hennigan, R. Interview with the author. Virtual. August 23, 2022.

Kanungo, S. Interview with the author. Virtual. July 7, 2022.

Karp, G. Interview with the author. Virtual. June 20, 2022.

Quinlan, C. Interview with the author. Virtual. June 30, 2022.

Sutherland, L. Interview with the author. Virtual. July 21, 2022.

9. Leadership behavior blueprint #3: Building trust

Blankson, A. Interview with the author. Virtual. July 20, 2022.

Cheney, T. Interview with the author. Virtual. June 3, 2022.

Cisło, A. Interview with the author. Virtual. June 22, 2022.

Crino, C. Interview with the author. Virtual. June 24, 2022.

Finnwards: Thriving in Finland. 'Remote work is here to stay?' February 17, 2022. www.finnwards.com/working-in-finland/remote-work-is-here-to-stay/

Gabriel, A. Interview with the author. Virtual. July 14, 2022.

Gill, S. Interview with the author. Virtual. July 7, 2022.

Karp, G. Interview with the author. Virtual. June 20, 2022.

Kondo, M., and Sonenshien, S. *Joy at work: Organizing your professional life.* New York: Little, Brown Spark, 2020.

Mistry, C. Interview with the author. Virtual. June 27, 2022.

Savage, M. 'Why Finland leads the world in flexible work.' August 8, 2019. BBC Worklife. www.bbc.com/worklife/article/ 20190807-why-finland-leads-the-world-in-flexible-work

Sobbott, S. Interview with the author. Virtual. July 7, 2022.

Thomas International remote working pledge, via Sabby Gill. Interview with the author. Virtual. July 7, 2022.

Thörner, V. Interview with the author. Virtual. August 26, 2022.

YLE News. 'Survey: Finland ranks #1 in citizen trust.' June 23, 2018. https://yle.fi/news/3-10270981

10. Leadership behavior blueprint #4: Setting boundaries

Cheney, T. Interview with the author. Virtual. June 3, 2022.

Hawley, S. Interview with the author. Virtual. August 23, 2022.

Lebre, M. 'Why you should be working asynchronously in 2022.' Remote. https://remote.com/blog/why-you-should-be-doing-async-work

Miller, L. Interview with the author. Virtual. July 13, 2022.

Patel, V. Interview with the author. Virtual. June 20, 2022.

Thörner, V. Interview with the author. Virtual. August 26, 2022.

11. Leadership behavior blueprint #5: Managing performance

Cheney, T. Interview with the author. Virtual. June 3, 2022.

Karp, G. Interview with the author. Virtual. June 20, 2022.

Loom International. 'Sawubona!' www.loominternational.org/sawubona/

Sakaguchi, J. Interview with the author. Virtual. July 22, 2022.

Sutherland, L. Interview with the author. Virtual. July 21, 2022.

TED. 'The gift and power of emotional courage: Susan David.' February 20, 2018. Video, 16:48. www.youtube.com/watch?v=NDQ1Mi5I4rg

Conclusion

Freedom at Work Talks. 'All you need is love… at work? Sigal Barsade.' November 3, 2015. Video, 20:11. www.youtube.com/watch?v=sKNTyGW3o7E

Murph, D. Interview with the author. Virtual. July 14, 2022.

Appendix A: Low carbon strategies for remote work

Quito, A. 'Every Google search results in CO2 emissions. This real time data viz shows how much.' July 20, 2022. Quartz. https://qz.com/1267709/every-google-search-results-in-co2-emissions-this-real-time-dataviz-shows-how-much/

Travers, K. 'How to reduce the environmental impact of your next virtual meeting.' March 4, 2021. *MIT News.* https://news. mit.edu/2021/how-to-reduce-environmental-impact-next-virtual-meeting-0304

Appendix B: Diversity and inclusion considerations for remote work

Gill, S. Interview with the author. Virtual. July 7, 2022.

Irish Congress of Trade Unions. 'Ireland's new "right to disconnect": How it works.' www.ictu.ie/blog/irelands-new-right-disconnect-how-it-works

Mearian, L. 'Women, minorities less inclined to return to office, face "proximity bias".' March 9, 2022. *Computer World.* www.computerworld.com/article/3652592/women-people-of-color-less-likely-to-want-to-return-to-office.html

Rani, Y. Interview with the author. Virtual. August 22, 2022.

Sawatzky, R. Interview with the author. Virtual. August 22, 2022.

INDEX

ABOUT THE AUTHOR

Melissa Romo earned her MBA from the Yale School of Management, where she studied organizational behavior and leadership. She is a regular speaker for events around the world, including the Digital Marketing World Forum, Generation Success Breaking Barriers, and the B2B Marketing Podcast, and has been recognized as a global advertising and marketing '40 Over 40', 'Inspirational Woman of the Year', and 'Inclusive Leader'.

In her most recent role as VP of Global Marketing, she leads a globally dispersed team for a leading business-to-business cloud software firm and has managed remote employees for more than a decade. She is also the author of the historical novel *Blue-Eyed Son,* a WWII-era story about displacement and loss of national identity during times of war, and has been a contributing writer on travel and expatriatism for publications in the US, UK, and Poland. She and her Spanish-born husband live outside New York City with their two teenage sons and rescued Labrador.